# From Exclusion to Reciprocity

*"Learning from Success"*

Jona M. Rosenfeld

IN DIALOGUE WITH JEAN-MICHEL DEFROMONT

**Hamilton Books**

An Imprint of
Rowman & Littlefield
Lanham • Boulder • New York • Toronto • Plymouth, UK

**Copyright © 2017 by Hamilton Books**
4501 Forbes Boulevard, Suite 200, Lanham, Maryland 20706
Hamilton Books Acquisitions Department (301) 459-3366

Unit A, Whitacre Mews, 26-34 Stannary Street,
London SE11 4AB, United Kingdom

All rights reserved
Printed in the United States of America
British Library Cataloguing in Publication Information Available

Library of Congress Control Number: 2016938860
ISBN: 978-0-7618-6798-2 (pbk : alk. paper)—ISBN: 978-0-7618-6799-9 (electronic)

∞™ The paper used in this publication meets the minimum requirements of American National Standard for Information Sciences Permanence of Paper for Printed Library Materials, ANSI/NISO Z39.48-1992.

To my parents, Johanna and Julius Rosenfeld,
who, together, and each in their own way,
accompany me on my personal and professional journey.

# Contents

| | |
|---|---|
| Preface | ix |
| Introduction | xiii |
| Note | xv |

**I: My Origins**     1
    1. The Beginning of Life: Six Weeks in a Hospital     1
    2. A Father to Follow     3
    3. The Ways of my Mother     8
    Notes     11

**II: Formative Years 1933–1955— From an Immigrant in Palestine to a Citizen of Israel**     13
    1. My Beginnings in Palestine     13
    2. Moving on: Training for Social Work in Post-War London     18
    3. My first assignment: When the Army is a Place for More than just Waging War     23
    4. Well-Baby Centers in Jerusalem: Being there at the Beginnings     26
    Notes     30

**III: Six Years in Chicago: "Unleashing Hidden Potential"\* on Learning the Craft of Social Work**     33
    Introduction: Learning the Craft of Social Work from the Past and for the Future     33
    1. On Becoming the Social Worker I became at the School of Social Service Administration in Chicago     35
    2. To Be a Social Worker One Needs to Overcome the "Strangeness between Helper and Client"     36

3. To Serve the Excluded in our Midst Requires the "Invention of Interventions" — 40
4. When an Outsider who Belongs Initiates Moves Beyond Exclusion — 42
5. Serving the Individual and the Collective: An Irresolvable Dilemma that Leads to Learning — 46
6. On Psychoanalysis and Social Work as the Key for Initiating Personal and Professional Reciprocity in the Present and thus for the Future — 47
Notes — 51

**IV: On Trails towards "Learning from Success": Seven Examples** — **53**
Introduction: Seven Pursuits which in Retrospect was an Unexpected Precursor of "Learning from Success" — 53
1. Training of Air Force Pilots in Israel (1954-55): How to Put an End to Excessive Flunking of Cadets — 54
2. Serving Families of Sailors in the Israeli Merchant Marine, 1964 — 55
3. The Unpredicted Mobility of Boys from a Low-Income Community: Which Patterns of Parenting Made their Resiliency Possible? — 57
4. When a Crisis is an Opportunity: What Enabled New York Families whose Homes Burned down to Achieve a Better Life — 58
5. On Forced Evacuations: From Sinai (1982) and then the Gaza Strip (2005) — 61
6. "To Be a 'Good Enough' Parent": How Nurses in Well-Baby Centers in Israel Implement a Learning Program Addressing Early Childhood Neglect if not Abuse (Rosenfeld, 2010) — 66
7. "Out from Under": A First Study on "Learning from the Success of Organizations Serving Socially Deprived Families in Israel" (Rosenfeld, 1992) (Rosenfeld, Schön and Sykes, 1995) — 72
Notes — 75

**Part V: Moving beyond Exclusion Means Initiating and Introducing Reciprocity** — **77**
1. On the Move from Exclusion to Reciprocity and how to Facilitate it — 77
2. On the Learning of Practices that Facilitate the Move from Exclusion to Reciprocity — 79

**VI: The Evolving of Reciprocity: The Long Journey of Chaim Who Survived the Holocaust at the Age of Three**     83
   Postscript     87

**VII: My Acquaintance with ATD* the Fourth World Movement: Where the Introduction of Reciprocity Is a Means for Moving Beyond Exclusion**     89
   Introduction: On Initiating Reciprocity and Ongoing Learning     89
   1. It's People Living in Poverty, Not Poverty     92
   2. How I got to Know the ATD Fourth World Movement: "The Man who was Shushed"     93
   3. "Emergence from Extreme Poverty": "So you Want to Know about the Successes of the Families"     95
   4. "Artisans of Democracy": What Might "Learning Companions" do to Enable Organizations to Contribute to Moves Beyond Exclusion     97
   5. From Learning that "Only the Best is 'Good Enough'" to Introducing the 17$^{th}$ of October— The World Day for the Eradication of Poverty— into the Knesset (Parliament) of Israel     99
   6. Learning for Action in an International Seminar Sponsored by the ATD Fourth World Movement     103
   7. Reflective Ongoing Learning from Success: A Chance for a Movement and Others with a Mission of Change     109
   Notes     110

**VIII: Epilogue: "Genocide" and "Poverty"—Two Collective Man-Made Evils of Our Epochs: A Challenge for the Future***     113

Acknowledgments     119

Appendix I ATD ("All Together in Dignity")— The Fourth World Movement*     121

Appendix II The Unit for Learning from Success and Ongoing Learning in Human Services, Myers-JDC-Brookdale Institute     123
   1. The Unit     123
   2. The Approach to Learning— "Learning from Success"     124

Appendix III The Three Methods of Learning from Success     127
   *The First Method:* The Retrospective Method—Learning from Past Successes     127
   *The Second Method*: The Prospective Method—Learning with and from a Learning Question     128

| | |
|---|---:|
| *The Third Method*: The Reflective Method— Learning on Learning in and from Action | 128 |
| Appendix IV The Components of the First and the Second Methods of Learning from Past Success | 129 |
| *First Method*: The Retrospective Method— Learning from Past Success | 129 |
| *Second Method*: The Prospective Method— Learning with and From Learning Questions | 131 |
| References | 135 |
| Index | 141 |

# Preface

At once, both intimately personal and thoroughly professional, this book is a vivid testimony to Jona Rosenfeld's life and his life's work. He was born in Germany and in 1933 immigrated with his family to Palestine, now Israel. He studied Colonial Social Science, then Psychiatric Social Work at the London School of Economics. After that he completed a BA in Sociology and Education at the Hebrew University in Jerusalem and then an MA and Ph.D. at the School for Social Service Administration at the University of Chicago.

His profession was social work but his life's work was dedicated to initiating and practicing what was for the benefit of the most unseen, "un[der]served," the excluded in our midst. He was trained in psychoanalytically-oriented psychotherapy, from which the "un[der]served" were not easily able to benefit. In those terms, the book is a fine blend of the personal and the professional—the man and his work.

Much of this he was able to accomplish by following in the footsteps of the family into which he was born. As he states in the book, he has no doubt that his highly impressive and daring family has been of primary importance in the way he has built his life. His parents were attuned to their times, as well as able and ready to daringly act on what they perceived to be right. His parents and his brothers had the foresight and the commitment to courageously pave their own ways in the nascent society and then the State of Israel. To a large degree this is what provided him with the courage and commitment required to pave his own way and to shape his own life and work.

He became a social worker not by choice, but an opportunity came his way after World War II. It did not take him long to make his mark on a field that was still in its infancy. With his drive, determination and creativity, he was able to take part in developing and shaping the field of social work to the needs of the time, and not according to the conventions of the profession elsewhere. His contribution to it emerged as a learner, thinker and inventor, which enabled him not to adhere to what social work had been in the past. Moreover, rather than being taken by surprise, he looked to address the continuously evolving situations from an original perspective. He was always ready to focus on what emerged, as an opportunity for acting and thus becoming, and not as a basis for explanation. What is especially noteworthy in this context, is the parallel emergence of the social work of Israel and Jona Rosenfeld the person. His contribution to social work was indeed relevant to the times. This might have contributed to his gaining both international recognition as a pioneer in different fields, as well as becoming the first recipient of the Israel Prize in Social Work.

Following one of Karl Marx's grand maxims, Chris Argyris is quoted as saying: "there are people who want to explain the world and others who want to change it, I want to change it." Argyris was set on changing the world for its benefit, and in this book it is for contribution to the un[der]served in our midst. Theory was less important to him as long as it did not serve those most in need. It is the affecting of change which is the central theme of this book as well as being the driving force behind its author. It may well be that because of this Rosenfeld did not see psychotherapy as the focus of his work, and viewed social work as an opportunity to specialize in a wide range of social issues. Hence his foci were, on the one hand, on "the invention of interventions" and on the other, on developing a methodology for "learning from success," i.e. to systematically deploy what had worked in the past as a basis for use in the present and thus for the future. Doing so is in line with the title of the book, to invest in paving ways for resolving previously unknown and, at least on the face of it, irresolvable issues. This also includes the "invention of interventions," the "merging of knowledge," and detracting from multiple "stake holders," modes of how to do so. Beyond all these, he had the idea of introducing on "reciprocity-based" modes of serving the "un[der]served," by "each becoming, at one and the same time the other's benefactor and beneficiary." It is this reciprocity that has the potential to pave the way for the excluded in our midst who, by definition, have been condemned to live in isolation, and thus to be introduced into society with multiple resources.

Seizing the opportunity to translate his vision into reality, Rosenfeld aligned himself with ATD The Fourth World Movement, which joins families living in extreme poverty and exclusion. He learned how their many activities in various locations around the world had enriched his and others people's work in the fight against poverty. In the book, a report on a Fair organized in the late 1980s by ATD at the Trocadero in Paris, together with people living in poverty, most beautifully captures the essence of the work of this Movement—both how they enable people to move out of poverty and together to learn how to do so.

Besides the fascinating personal stories, the book abounds with accounts of initiatives and examples of programs implemented and events attended. To crown it all, the book ends with a call to address two unaddressed manmade evils: genocide and poverty, both world-wide challenges for the future. This also affirms Rosenfeld's optimism and deep belief that "things can get better" where both learning and generosity are present.

It was in line with this that Rosenfeld established the Unit of Learning from Success and Ongoing Learning in Human Services at the Myers-JDC-Brookdale Institute of Research in Jerusalem in 1995. This both to develop the three Methods of Learning from Success and to accompany organizations and initiatives interested in including "learning from success" as part of their work and to disseminate them.

Finally, it is important to mention that it is thanks to the partnership with Jean-Michel Defromont, already for many years a member of the "Permanent Volontariat," which is part of the ATD Fourth World Movement addressing families living in extreme poverty, this joint work would not have been possible. Jean-Michel's contribution was essential. On the one hand, his generosity, authenticity and commitment were inspirational. On the other, his availability and his belonging to this extremely unusual and inspiring ATD Fourth World Movement were essential to this whole project.

# Introduction

If you strike up a conversation with almost anyone about learning from success the reaction will usually be one of surprise since we usually associate learning from and with failure, i.e. from knowledge gained from mistakes. Indeed, the latter learning process is the more common one, both in the field of scholarship and in popular opinion. In this volume I shall assume that we can actually learn much more from past successes, i.e. from what had worked in the past, than from failures. But the latter leaves us with what this learning consists of and how do we link this learning at the individual level with that of learning in institutions and societies?

Whatever may have been my previous interest in this subject, it was around 2009 that I was invited by the Delegation General of the International ATD Fourth World Movement[1], an organization with a world-wide concern for families living in extreme poverty and exclusion, to write this book with its three different facets: (1) my checkered life story as a citizen of Israel and beyond it; (2) my ever-changing pursuits and conceptions of what social work is all about; (3) finally, the decidedly important role that the 40-year-connection with ATD Fourth World Movement has played in my life and work.

In bringing together and organizing these diverse strands, I took up the issue of the move beyond exclusion or "roads beyond exclusion". This issue is a central theme of this book. The heart of it being that what happens once one has initiated, introduced, if not established "roads beyond exclusion". This means, after having established "reciprocal relations", where each is a beneficiary and a benefactor as each being a first and generative step beyond exclusion. The latter is very much in tune with the work of ATD Fourth World Movement, as with my view of the profession of social work. It is this unusual Movement's commitment to persons living in poverty in different countries and to the topic of poverty which is so relevant for social work and especially to the "craft" of social work. It was on the basis of my understanding of this, not by chance international movement, that had enabled me to discover and redefine what the domain and expertise of social work is (Rosenfeld, 1983). It is in this sense that ATD Fourth World Movement and social work are sharing together, a not always clearly explicated common vision and mission which is also reflected in the additional title of this book: "Learning from Success" in addition to "From Exclusion to Reciprocity". Both of these are of crucial relevance in many spheres of my interest. These latter wide-ranging themes do, in a unique way, also integrate my interest in psychotherapy and psychoanalysis, the mission of social work, the work of ATD Fourth World Movement and my own personal life.

Thus, if there is one point that underlies much of both my professional and personal life, is that of introducing reciprocity, the mutual exchange of views and perspectives and the doing it together on the one hand and being safely together, on the other. Having in mind one idea which I have learned from ATD—"Don't talk *at* me but *with* me"—constitutes one illustration of what I have been able to benefit from the ATD Fourth World Movement, from its late founder Père Joseph Wresinski and from its unusual membership, have achieved. They have shown what can so easily be forgotten and which was noted centuries ago, i.e. that from amongst the poorest wisdom will, and can, emanate. That understanding too has been made real in how throughout the world, ATD Fourth World Movement has been able to transform "engaging with poverty" into "engaging with people and families *living in poverty*", and this, as such, as a universal, cross-national phenomenon. It is for that reason that they consider themselves a movement and not an organization.

In this vein, I want to acknowledge my profound thanks for having been given the opportunity to contribute to what is common to both our respective mission and vision—that of ATD Fourth World Movement and of social work. The social work profession and ATD Fourth World Movement have much to show and much to learn from each other in making this conception a reality and so, as a guide for thought and action.

If that were not enough, it is also connected to my gladly having received in 1998, the first Israel Prize for Research in Social Work.

For this reason I was particularly pleased to be able to share with the ATD Fourth World Movement the concept of "learning from success" and to deploy it as a means for identifying their actionable principles in the course of a series of both joint learning events and different publications.

I am very grateful for having been able to mobilize in this effort the Unit for Learning from Success and Ongoing Learning in Human Services that I established at the Myers-JDC Brookdale Institute in 1995. I want to thank the

Institute for its full enthusiastic embracing of this work and to my partners in that unit who were an integral part of making it happen.

To all this, I also need to add that at the age of forty nine I married my very special partner and wife Ruti and that we have two daughters, Noa and Yael. So far we have five grandchildren: Noa's and Ilan's children Yotam, Shira, Yair and Avigail; Elliott's and Yael's son Oren. I have been very fortunate and continue to be so in that sphere of my life as well.

## NOTE

1. See Appendix I.

# I

# My Origins

## 1. THE BEGINNING OF LIFE: SIX WEEKS IN A HOSPITAL

I have always known that soon after my cesarean delivery (on November 30, 1922) I, the youngest of three brothers in a Jewish family in Germany, stayed for six weeks in a hospital where I was looked after by Catholic nurses. I also still remember being told that the head of the hospital was a Doctor Lust (yes, "lust"), who later remained our pediatrician, and that my mother sent her breast milk to the hospital for me every evening. She had not been able to visit me then because of her post-partum condition and her diabetes.

My father told me about his visits there, at times on his own and sometimes with my brothers. The reason for my extended hospitalization was that I suffered from an illness called "pyloric stenosis" which, as I later found out, is a disease that is more common in male children. I also learned that this disease had the colorful name, Magenpfoertnerkrampf, literally "the cramp of the guardian of the stomach". It is an illness of the muscles which prevents food from being held down and which causes excessive vomiting. The cure was gradual spoon-feeding, which the nurses did and which enabled the malfunctioning muscle to gradually acquire the ability to hold down food.

Perhaps another noteworthy component of this first experience and one which I remember hearing repeatedly was that four months later, on my mother's first birthday following my birth, my father and brothers rolled my cradle into her bedroom with a bunch of violets in my hands and with a written note which said, "look how clever your son is, he can already present you with violets". Later on I often reflected that my father may have wished to convey not so much that I was that clever as that I could do something for my mother so early on. These kinds of stories have contributed, I believe, to my later awareness of what young children can do for their parents at an early age and that in these terms, all kinds of reciprocity was really there from the beginning.

And then there was Elisabeth Roberts, my memorable Christian Kinderfraeulein (nursemaid), with whom I enjoyed a relationship of reciprocity that always meant so much to me. Elisabeth was with me and for me when my parents were away, which happened quite often, such as when they traveled to Jerusalem to the opening of the Hebrew University in 1925, when I was two and a half years old. I remember the times that she took me, a Jewish boy, to the entrance steps of her church and once to a nearby village where her family lived, not in order to convert me but rather because children were important to her and—as I now understand—gave meaning to her life too. Later, one evening and without warning, Elisabeth stepped into my room, led by my mother who told me that when I woke up the next day Elisabeth would be gone. She was going to look after other children in a Deaconess nunnery in a city named Essen, which means "eating". This caused me to wonder whether she went there to feed them, which might well have made me envious of them. Elisabeth explained there and then how from then on our eyes would meet whenever we looked at the same stars at night, even if we were far away from each other. I can still see Elisabeth receding into the background, and from that night on and for several years afterwards I tried to connect with her through the stars but never saw her again. She sent one postcard which I remember, and some years ago when I was sixty, I sent a letter of inquiry to the city authorities of Essen, trying to trace someone called Elisabeth Roberts among its inhabitants. The answer was negative.

Elisabeth used to sing with me (a young boy from a Jewish family in Karlsruhe in the south of Germany), a Christian prayer which I can still sing:

> Deine Gunst und Jesu Blut,
> Machen allen Schaden Gut
> (Your kindness and the blood of Jesus
> Will do away with any damage)

Later on, my mother often reminded me that in my singing I mispronounced it as "Jaden" (a word that does not exist in German) instead of "Schaden", i.e. "damage" which I must have felt was too serious to be joked about. Whatever else this may have implied, it highlighted the fact that these, "her" Christian songs were there to accompany me in our Jewish home, not as something to be feared or denigrated but with an openness to other cultures that characterized my parents.

Throughout my life, Elisabeth's spirit has accompanied me in many other ways, including perhaps in my lifelong interest in the lives of young children and in parent-child relationships. Indeed, I have often wondered whether this might explain why, as a night watchman in Kibbutz Ginossar, long before I had my own children but twenty years after losing Elisabeth, I was drawn to the Baby House in which the children slept. (According to the ideology of the Kibbutz Movement, children of the kibbutz did not sleep in their parents' homes.) Whenever I heard a child crying while I was on guard duty, I would go to the home of the child's parents to alert them to the crying and suggest that they go and comfort their child. I thought about Elisabeth too when my late friend Israel Katz, a social worker who later became an Israeli Minister of Welfare, mentioned in one of his speeches that: "as long as there is one child who cries at night and nobody hears him, ours is not a humane society". And indeed, surely the connection to Elisabeth at least partially explains my life's work in Well-Baby Clinics in Israel, to which I will return later. It may well be that, for all this, I found meaning in how T.S. Eliot (1940) began and ended "East Coker", one of his *Four Quartets:* "In my beginning is my end […] In my end is my beginning" (Eliot, 1943).

## 2. A FATHER TO FOLLOW

One day in 1939 (we had arrived in Israel in 1933), when I was about seventeen years old, I walked down Jaffa Street in Jerusalem with my father. Unexpectedly, he pointed across the street at a well-dressed man whom I didn't know. He said, "the man you see there is Dr. Simon. When I was about to marry your mother, that man went to see your grandfather to tell him not to allow his daughter Johanna to marry me, 'ecause my father—Julius—is a Zionist'[1] and not 'salonfaehig'"[2] . When I asked my father to explain, he told me that Dr. Simon was an assimilated Jew who thought that Jews should live like Germans and that Zionists (who believed in establishing a Jewish State in Palestine), were therefore not honorable enough to visit the "salons" of upper class German Jews and should be outcast. And, my father added, "there he is, walking in the streets of Jerusalem, in the Zionist country that saved his life." This was one of many examples of how my father taught us why Zionism was so essential and that thus being an outsider was nothing to fear nor to be embarrassed about.

The importance of Zionism in our lives was already apparent in the summer of 1925 when I was two and a half years old and, as I had mentioned, my parents went to the ceremony of the opening of the Hebrew University in Jerusalem. This was their first trip to Palestine and it was especially important to my father who had always wanted us to live there and who wanted to explore possibilities for doing so. For this reason and also because both of my parents were interested in intellectual issues, the idea of establishing a university in Jerusalem meant a great deal to both of them. My brothers Jakob and Immanuel and I stayed behind; I was looked after by my governess Elisabeth. I clearly remember, thanks to the story being repeated over and over again by my mother, that upon their return, I sat on my pot and said, "kenn's noch Mutti", a sentence that has a double meaning. It means both, "I remember you" and is also an inquiry, "do you remember me?" It still strikes me that I asked her if she remembered me rather than telling her that I still remembered her. Beyond that I clearly recall the off-white silken blouse with its blue embroidery—the color of the Zionist flag—which they gave me upon their return, as a present from Palestine. I still have a picture of me wearing this "Zionist" blouse made in Palestine, the country that later became our family's refuge and eventual homeland.

I also remember when one of my brother Immanuel's teachers, who later became a Nazi Governor of Paris, complained to my parents that when he had asked my brother what our father—who was a lawyer—did for a living, my brother said "he is a Zionist". Having identified him as a Zionist rather than a lawyer, made my father clearly proud of Immanuel's awareness of our father's Zionism. My father used to tell us often about how in 1905, when he was eighteen years old, he volunteered to serve as an orderly at the first Zionist Congress in Basel after the death of Theodor Herzl, the founder of the Zionist Movement. In that vein, my brother Jacob received for his "bar-mitzvah"[3] an original etching of Herzl by the well-known painter Herman Struck, himself a Zionist who later moved to Palestine and whose portrait is in our home today.

Sometimes, especially during the Jewish festivals, my father spoke to us about our responsibility as Jews to return to Palestine, the Land of Israel, and that we had to act and feel like Jews. What was often confusing for me were the differences between being Jewish, being a Zionist, and being a religious Jew. In our home, where we always felt that our lives in Germany were temporary in a country belonging to others, not our real homeland, being Jewish meant being Zionist Jews, who had to establish a Jewish State in Palestine, later Israel. In this respect, my father was bold in his desire to leave the comfortable surroundings of a middle-class life and realize his dream of living in the Jewish homeland to which we did not truly belong. Perhaps this too gave meaning to the name of this book and the road we took later to a place that during the 1920s and 1930s was seen at best as little more than a "primitive" backwater far from European civilization.

Even before that, all of us knew that the blue-and-white Keren Kayemet (Jewish National Fund) box in our sitting room was for collecting money that served the Zionist Movement that was buying land in Palestine and that every Sunday morning my brothers received Hebrew lessons. At this time my brothers were already members of "Kadima" ("Going forward" in Hebrew), a Zionist Youth Movement, which I too later joined. Hence, it was not by chance that upon our move to Berlin when I was seven, I was sent to its first and only Zionist school.

One particularly memorable aspect in the life of our family was the customary Jewish celebration of Tu B'shvat—the 15th of the Hebrew month Shvat. There, in the middle of the winter, we ate fifteen types of fruit to celebrate this holiday named the "Birthday of the Trees". While in Germany this felt quite out of place, in the spring in Palestine as I later experienced it, the timing made perfect sense. At that time, the holiday reminded us that there was another world, another country-the Land of Israel in which it was already springtime and a place quite different from Germany with its wintery weather. This was a wondrous occurrence, which by being so puzzling made us aware that there would be many surprises in store for us. It thus gave us a foretaste of the unique meaning Zionism would hold for us in the future.

All of these understandings—that for me were often unarticulated—peaked and crystallized as I began to comprehend the vital implications of Zionism, when one evening in January 1933 we stood on the balcony of our apartment, on the fifth floor of our home in Berlin, and down below marched thousands of Nazis with torches in their hands singing a song whose words I still remember:

> Wenn's Judenblut vom Messer spritzt, dann geht's nochmal so gut [When the blood of the Jews drip down from the knives, everything will be better].

This song—part of the Nazi Hymn, "Sturmsoldaten-Lied"—has been indelibly printed on my mind ever since I heard it at the age of ten, and because soon after that night my family began to dissolve.

First my brother Jacob, then 18 years old, left for Palestine where he became a lifelong member of Kibbutz Giv'at-Brenner, despite his original plans to return to Berlin to study medicine. Then on one Friday, on the eve of the Saturday Boycott Day, the day on which the Nazi government publicly declared it forbidden to do business with Jews, we accompanied my father to a Berlin railway station on his way to The Hague. He went to work for a business owned by Jews with a branch in Holland. The owner of the company, who left together with my father, went to stay there with his family, and his company was later transferred to The Hague. My father left because he was afraid of what would happen to him at the hands of the Nazi government and soon afterwards he decided that all of us would emigrate to Palestine. In the wake of these developments, shortly after my father's departure, my brother Immanuel, then sixteen, also went to Holland to live with a peasant family to learn about agriculture, which would later serve him well when he too arrived in Palestine.

Then, when only my mother and I remained in Berlin, most of our possessions were auctioned. The only ones which we kept were those that had been packed and shipped to Palestine. I remember being quite upset by the crowds of strangers in our apartment who bought our belongings. I especially remember the moment they stood to auction off a small gold-colored statue of three little bulldogs. In a panic I begged my mother not to let this happen, and she rescued those dogs who later accompanied us to our new home in Jerusalem.

With our home dissolved, my mother traveled to meet my father and brother in Holland after having deposited me—a ten-year-old—in a Jewish children's home near Berlin named "Caput", which sounds like but is not spelled "Kaput" which means "broken". I hated that place so much that after two days, after I had broken both a mirror and a soup tureen, and in spite of having been told that the person we could hear playing the violin was Albert Einstein, I took my suitcase, walked to the railway station and went to stay with one of our Zionist relatives in Berlin. At my request, they phoned both Caput and my parents to inform them that I had safely arrived at their home. Then, soon after my mother returned, she told me that my father had left Holland for Palestine and described her tearful parting from my brother Immanuel at the railway station in Deventer in Holland.

A few weeks later, my mother and I set out on our way to Palestine. Around that time I had to take leave of my Zionist school in Berlin which had really been a haven that sheltered me from what was happening in Germany. In August 1933, we traveled by train to Basel and my memories of that journey include my mother knitting, something she had rarely done before, and my cheerfully informing her whenever the custom officers entered our compartment. These moments caused her great anxiety because she knew, as I did not, that our money was hidden in the balls of wool. On the way we said goodbye to our relatives in Basel, and to Tante Frieda Fromm-Reichmann, then in Montana Vermala, took the SS Roma from Genoa to Naples, where we visited Pompeii, and from there onto Athens where we visited the Acropolis. Each of these stops—described in letters my father had written to us on his travels to Palestine—became additional milestones on our way there several months later.

It was early in the morning of the fifteenth of September 1933 (a day I mark every year)—on the eve of the Jewish New Year—that we arrived in the port of Haifa, on a very hot day. I remember how we queued up on the ship when every so often someone would jump to the deck below to avoid the line and leave the ship faster. I remember how, as it got later and later, I told my mother that, "I always knew I would never see my father again". My mother seemed puzzled and a bit impatient with my impatience, and told me so. In the end it was over ten hours after landing when, at long last, I saw my father and my brother Jacob waiting on the dockside. So I did see him again but when we met I was totally speechless. It took me several days to believe that he really was there, and much longer than that to really reconnect with him and see him, my father, in the Land of Zion, a real place, not merely an image or a dream.

As T.S. Eliot (1943) wrote: "Home is where one starts from" and indeed, for the first time, I remember my sense of having arrived at home.

It is not by chance that at this juncture I am reminded about parting from my father fifteen years later, around the time of his death in 1949. This was after we had lived a good life for twelve years in Palestine and after I had come back from studying in London. Upon returning in the summer of 1948, in the besieged city of Jerusalem during a few days of a truce during the War of Independence, I saw that my father was terminally ill. That I could go there together with my brother Immanuel was only thanks to a letter which my late friend Yehoshua Neuberger, later Ramot, who was working in the Headquarters of the Medical Corps, wrote: "This letter requests permission for Dr. Rosenfeld and his assistant to visit Jerusalem". Dr. Rosenfeld was me, who of course had no doctorate and my "assistant" was my brother Immanuel. A few weeks later when I again returned to Jerusalem to take my father by ambulance to Tel Aviv, we took our last walk down Jaffa Street both knowing he was nearing the end of his life. We did so silently and sadly because each one in his own way knew how much the street and this city meant to him. For me it was a road I would follow and have continued to follow even without him, ever since our reunion in 1933. For him this was the end of his life's journey. For me this was the beginning of my life in Palestine, later Israel.

When my father died three months later, it began to sink in that in contrast to our earlier separation in 1933, this time I really would never see him again. It then became clear to me how many of the roads I had taken were paved by my father. The roads taken by him were very clear and the roads to be followed by me became increasingly so. In retrospect, I would say that I have followed my father in my own ways of being and working—with the difficulties he faced but with his readiness to be an outsider (Rosenfeld, 2015), and like him to follow through and act on my beliefs. I have also come to understand my mother's unique contribution to my life, as will become clear in the next section, since through her I learned to be deeply committed to making my own choices. It was my mother who also enabled me to carry out this commitment while remaining connected to what had happened in the past. In addition, and perhaps unintentionally, the many separations from my parents allowed me later in my life to more readily empathize with those left behind at the margins of societies. This too so clearly reflects how both of my parents, each in their own way, have so clearly contributed to me, and that it was that that had enabled me to endeavor to follow each and both in my own way.

All these memories are accompanied by indelible recollections of my father playing the cello, my mother the piano, both singing, on Saturday evenings when they played chamber music next to my bedroom. I also clearly remember the celebration of Jewish holidays including, attending synagogue and the comings and goings of members of the family and friends. We three brothers were so clearly included in it all that we could not but feel throughout our lives that that was the "home we started from", where each of us was seen and heard each in terms of his own personal interests and potential. For example, my parents allowing my older brother, just sixteen, to go on holiday with a girlfriend, and encouraging my second brother to pursue his interest in playing the piano. For myself, I have no doubt that this home was a "launching pad" that enabled me to pursue and believe that "only the best is good enough". This is an expression which I heard when I met the Fourth World Movement and what they thought was clearly for the poorest of the poor. In time I understood that this idea was not only for the likes of me but also for those who were and are excluded from our midst, whose predominant quests might also be for reciprocity, for both receiving *and* contributing.

To end this section, let me mention that when during my early years my father said that Zionism meant "amor fati" or to "love one's fate", I was ready to do so because I understood it as "amor Vati" which meant "love thy father". My father was indeed an upright person, tender towards others, who could also be firm. He would do what he believed he should even if it meant being an outsider and would withdraw into himself when things became too much for him. With all this, my father was not someone who would urge others to follow him, but when they did, it was on their own initiative.

It was not by chance that when, at my first Group Relations Conference on Authority and Leadership at the Tavistock Institute, one of its staff—Brendan Duddy from Northern Ireland—said good-bye to me by saying, "Good-bye Mr. Rosenfeld and I am glad that you knew how to choose your father", and on this I will say some more at the end of the book.

So I may rightly mention here that I had learned from success that moving on is not only possible but can well lead beyond exclusion.

### 3. THE WAYS OF MY MOTHER

> " . . . To say the things he truly feels and not the words of one who kneels. The record shows I took the blows and did it my way!"[4]

My mother, Johanna née Ettlinger, was a formidable person, whose mother was born to a Ukrainian aristocratic Jewish family, and was both intelligent and beautiful. She, like my father and then me, was born in Karlsruhe, Germany. She was the first-born daughter to a Jewish orthodox couple. Her mother Amelie nee Brotzki, born in the Ukraine, and her modest and tender father Jonas, after whom I was named two years after his death. Following her came three sons, Felix, Karl and Siegfried. My mother's father and my paternal grandfather were both named Jona and both their marriages had been match-made. My grandmother Amelie too was a highly intelligent and impressive woman who, while still a girl, had fled with her mother, my great grandmother Berta-Bejlsche, from the Ukraine to Germany in the 1880's, to seek freedom from her husband's my maternal grandfather's, mental illness. Later, after the First World War, in 1919, my grandmother Amelie became a teacher of Russian, English and French, giving private lessons to university students because inflation forced her to earn money at a time when there were few Jewish women who were able to do so.

My mother was the "princess" of the family and adored by her father. She sang, played the piano, participated in reading circles of German literature and was sent to a "Pensionat", a boarding school for daughters of upper-class Jewish families. In contrast to their parents, my mother and father married by choice.

I remember that my mother, who was tall, beautiful, and a bit heavy, was not one to shy away from voicing her opinions. One Shabbat, at the bar-mitzvah of my brother Jakob, sitting in the middle of the first row in the upper floor reserved for the women in the synagogue, she suddenly, in the midst of the rabbi's sermon, got up, and stalked out in protest. In the courtyard, surrounded by my father, members of the family and by some others who had followed her out, she delivered an intense discourse of which I was not then able to make head or tail. All I saw was that she was the life and soul of that odd "party". I later understood that in his sermon the rabbi had compared Zionism to blasphemy. He preached that "when" in the first generation there is a sin of blasphemy, in the second, there will be fratricide. This was his way of protesting against my parents' Zionism. Several years later, I witnessed my parents' sense of victory, when that same rabbi after having been rescued from the Nazis, had found rescue and served as a rabbi in the "Land of Zion"—Palestine.

This was the first of many times I remember seeing my mother, in all her majesty, captivating others with her wisdom, charisma and daring. Over the years I came to realize how many eminent and remarkable men and women sought her counsel, among them writers, politicians and lawyers. They came to see her because she communicated with them in a way that allowed them to reflect upon their lives, the challenges they faced and the disagreements they had with other people. In addition, one of her outstanding characteristics was a capacity and a commitment to engage others in talking about meaningful issues. This did not stop her from being critical and not always tolerant, especially of those who did not do what they had promised to do.

I believe that what I most knowingly respected in my mother was her deep interest in humanistic pursuits such as literature or music and her dedication to the psychoanalytic point of view. This was perhaps because she was someone who needed to be consistent and to live up to what she and her circle of friends and family were committed to. Perhaps that too explains her readiness to undergo psychoanalytic therapy which few men, and even fewer women, of her generation dared to do. Indeed, there were not many people who, in that period, the mid 1920's, underwent analytic treatment as she did, and which later on my father did as well. She often went to nearby Baden Baden to see Dr. Georg Groddeck (Groddeck, 1928), the well-known psychiatrist and the originator of the word "Das Es" (the It) which Freud introduced into the vocabulary of psychoanalysis. My mother's interest in psychoanalysis and in the unconscious centered around "knowing oneself". And without necessarily doing so consciously, she acted as someone for whom being such a person is an ultimate value. In those terms my mother and father complemented each other and this connected them both to my father's cousin "Tante Frieda", the well-known psychoanalyst Frieda Fromm-Reichmann, the Dr. Freed appearing in "I Never Promised you a Rose Garden" (Greenberg, 1964). In fact, it is worth reminding ourselves of the climax of that book as it serves as an example of my mother's vision. The book is about an adolescent patient with a psychosis, who had invented a language of her own which her analyst learned in order to help her. Then, when she was on her way to leave the hospital and rejoin the world, she witnessed a nurse hitting a patient. Approaching Dr. Freed, she asked, "is that the world you want me to rejoin?" Whereupon Dr. Freed says, "I never promised you a rose garden . . . I only promised you to understand", by which she implied that being well, the opposite of being psychotic, comes from knowing oneself without having control over the world.

My first real understanding of what psychoanalysis is all about came during my adolescence. During this period I had the opportunity to read the many books on psychoanalysis which my parents had in their library. At that time the seeds were planted for my continuing commitment to psychoanalysis as a means of being and becoming who one is, following what Polonius advised Laertes in Shakespeare's "Hamlet", "This above all: to thine own self be true, And it must follow, as the night the day. Thou canst not then be false to any man." These lines have remained with me throughout my life. Further on I will explore how this is also connected to my deep belief that anyone—even the poorest of the poor and the mentally ill—can be able to use and benefit from knowing themselves however unaware of their unconscious they might be. Being aware of one's unconscious never was a societal norm but it was one I had strived to do and not as an elitist insight into psychoanalysis but something that can be applied also to more marginalized, sections of society.

I have many people to thank for becoming increasingly able to acknowledge and stay actively committed to what psychoanalysis has to offer, primarily as a way to know oneself (and not as a doctrine). But I acknowledge that it was my mother who initially inspired me to dare as she had throughout her own life, and thus enabled me to see awareness of the unconscious as an opportunity, whether painful or fulfilling.

Ultimately, understanding the differences in the kinds and levels of autonomy vested in my father's Zionism and my mother's psychoanalysis has enabled me to accomplish much of what I have struggled for in both my personal and my professional life. In other words, the readiness to know oneself and to act upon that knowledge—the very essence of being autonomous—should be at the heart of the choices we make, and thus the aim of social work, in turn, is to provide the means for making such autonomous choices by any member of society, and to learn from success on how to pave one's own road beyond exclusion and to accompany the others to pave their own.

## NOTES

1. This refers to my father having been a member of the Zionist Movement founded by Theodor Herzl in Europe with the idea that the future of Jews was to be the establishment of a Zionist State in Palestine. My father, who was studying Law, was a member of the Zionist Student Movement K.J.V.—Kartell Juedischer Verbindungen—Cartel of Jewish Connectedness, which was an umbrella organization of Jewish Zionist students in Germany.

2. Not *"Fit for socially respectable society "* , (Oxford English Dictionary) ; literally not good enough for the salon of non-Zionist Jews in Germany.

3. *Bar-Mitzvah* is the term used to describe the day a Jewish boy is recognized in Judaism as an adult. The Bar-Mitzvah ceremony, during which the boy traditionally reads from the *Torah* and officially recites certain obligatory prayers, symbolizes the community's expectations of him as an adult.

4. "My Way" is a song popularized by Frank Sinatra. Its lyrics were written by Paul Anka and set to music based on the French song *"Comme d'habitude"* composed in 1967 by Claude François and Jacques Revaux, with lyrics by Claude François and Gilles Thibault. Anka's English lyrics are unrelated to the original French song.

*II*

# Formative Years 1933–1955 — From an Immigrant in Palestine to a Citizen of Israel

### 1. MY BEGINNINGS IN PALESTINE

In 1933 we landed in Palestine, the land to which we had immigrated in search of a home. Only in the years to come did it dawn on us that joining this society had saved our lives. The knowledge that we had escaped from a place where we did not belong and arrived in a place where we did belong, became an intrinsic driving force for my parents, my brothers, and me. We consciously responded to this recognition during the coming years, which were so clearly formative for me. These were years of struggle, of fulfilling one's duties, of answering the "call" of the emerging Jewish state without complaint yet without becoming blind followers. While often rough, these times were not without moments of elation, springing from an enormous sense of achievement in building a new society and from our country's growing capacity for self-defense.

This sense was somewhat tempered by the gnawing pain, born of our collective displacement of others—the Palestinians—and with it the mounting resentment and hatred between us and them. I remember that during my primary school years one of our teachers arranged for us to visit a nearby Arab school and they, in turn, reciprocated the visit. For a young ten-year-old boy such experiences turned seeing the Palestinians not as abstract objects but as persons. Thus later, when conflict emerged between the Jewish and

Arab communities of Palestine, my feelings, as those of my family, were mixed: while fearful of the Palestinians and worried about attacks, we also knew them as individuals and realized that they had their own justified views about actions undertaken by Jews. During the 1930s, moreover, our fear was allayed by the fact that Palestine was a British mandate which did and did seek out to restrain the mutual enmity between Jews and Arabs.

Our moments of joy and sense of success were inevitably interspersed with fear of defeat and annihilation and, in time, by a hovering cloud of sorrow related to the fate of those we left behind. In this vein, in 1937, when I was fifteen years old, my father urged his brother, "Onkel Karl" and his wife "Tante Liesel", to come from Germany to visit us for two weeks. My father had hoped to convince them to relocate to Palestine. Despite my father's hope of convincing them to move to Palestine with their two sons, Karl wanted to believe that he would be safe, even as a Jew in Nazi Germany, because he had lost a leg while serving in the German Army during World War I. At the end of their visit with us they agreed to come to Palestine and from that moment my father tried, to no avail, to obtain an immigration certificate for them. Upon their return to Germany, they started to make emigration arrangements, including sending their belongings to Marseille for shipment to Palestine. They had already sent one of their sons, the late George Rosney, to England and the other, the late Benyamin Ramot, to Palestine. But Karl and Liesel stayed behind and to our horror the two were forced from Karlsruhe to Stuttgart, then to the Theresienstadt Concentration Camp, and finally to the Auschwitz Extermination Camp. My father never forgave himself for not having been able to secure an immigration certificate for them.

I recalled all of this quite recently while reading a book called "The King's Most Loyal Enemy Aliens: Germans who Fought for Britain in the Second World War" (Fry, 2007) about Jewish soldiers in the British Army. In this book I found an account of Karl and Liesel's son, my cousin George, who at the end of the war, in 1945, went in search of his parents at Theresienstadt. Travelling by motorbike (given to him by his British commander) and hoping to find his parents there, he learned instead the awful truth, that they had been murdered in Auschwitz. The story of our family is in some ways quite unusual. In contrast to many others, most of our family came to Palestine and was saved, at least in part thanks to my father's Zionism. Because of his foresight, many members of our family escaped to Palestine before the war and in doing so also managed to emigrate with some financial resources and belongings, a factor that helped them to settle in more successfully than would have otherwise been the case. Helping newcomers to settle in was one of my father's main preoccupations during his life in Palestine.

I saw my father engaged in helping newcomers from Germany when, during the thirties and early forties, I would collect him every Friday at lunch time from his office at the Jerusalem German Immigrants Association. At that time, as head of the Association in Jerusalem, he held regular office hours during which he supported new immigrants from Germany and helped them to pave their way into Jerusalem society. I saw how caring he was with new immigrants who had come to a society in which they often felt lost. Beyond the formal position my father held, our house in Talpiot, on the outskirts of the city, was always a home for relatives and friends who were recent arrivals, many of them came to stay with us, some for shorter and others for longer periods of time.

My school years in Jerusalem, can be characterized by a verse we sang every Friday in my Secondary School: "To learn from the past what the future shall be". As a newcomer, I lived a privileged life, with both financial and educational advantages, as well as the benefit of emotional support, and I used these to bridge the gap between what had been and what would yet be. I endeavored to strike a balance between assimilating and adjusting, between completely giving up my previous identity and becoming just like any other Jew born in the country, or adding new aspects of the environment to what I had come with from Germany. On the one hand, I tried as quickly as possible to become integrated into a society where the common good was paramount, yet on the other hand, I wanted to hold on to my roots. Situated between these two forces left me somewhat of an outsider, albeit with enough space to become authentic and autonomous—to learn new things while retaining my values about what is right and wrong while respecting the values of others. In retrospect, I believe that I succeeded in maintaining a balance by acting as what I would now call a "loyal outsider". This role allowed me to maintain loyalty both to my current society, where I was growing up, but without letting that overshadow what I had brought with me. This balance enabled me at the time to pave my own way and has continued since then to serve me well (Rosenfeld, 2015).

I know now, in retrospect, that I would not have been able to act on my beliefs had it not been for the unquestioning support I received from my parents. As expounded earlier, my parents' home and my childhood were steeped in the values of both Zionism and Western culture. I grew up with an active interest in German, Hebrew and English literature, in theatre, in art and music, but also in psychoanalysis. Psychoanalysis became for me a challenge, which required one to be true and honest both with others and with oneself. It also expects and develops one's capacity to trust others, so as to be truly willing and able to benefit from them. With hindsight I can see that this in some ways foreshadowed my interest in the opportunities provided by "reciprocity" and reciprocal relationships, to which I shall refer throughout. Indeed, I believe that in this search for what I now call "reciprocity" I wanted to connect with others who could and would be there also for me. At the same time I wanted these to be people (and relationships) from whom I could not only truly benefit whatever their beliefs or personal characteristics but who were also ready that I would benefit from them if not them from me.

In this vein, during my high school years I connected with some unusual teachers, many of whom were new immigrants themselves, who later became well-known academics, who at the time had had no choice but to teach in a secondary school rather than at the Hebrew University, which was, at that time, the only university in Palestine. Because of their being true to who they were and the high caliber of their teaching I became fascinated with the Bible, reading it both as pure literature and as part of history. I also devoured the best of Hebrew, English and German literature as well as books on psychoanalysis and history, which, as I have stated, I found in my parents' home.

At that time I also had an unforgettable Hebrew teacher who helped me to overcome my difficulty mastering the Hebrew language, a challenge perhaps born of my reluctance to forgo my mother tongue and the home it represented. This teacher, a beautiful and gentle young woman named Fania Musman, who later became the mother of the now-famous Hebrew novelist Amoz Oz, inspired me and many of her other students "to write our life stories". With genuine interest, she invited me to share who and what I, somewhat of an outsider, was all about, and by doing so she helped me to feel truly welcome in our joint society. This was perhaps the first time I became explicitly aware of what it means to be an outsider even in a place to which one belongs. As a result, belonging is a theme I have continued to explore throughout my life, as will be revealed further in later sections.

In addition to being an eager student, I also traveled extensively around my new country, attending theaters and concerts and acting in plays on the stage. All this came to an end when, upon graduating from high school in 1941, I decided not to join the Jewish Brigade or the Palmach (elite, strike force of the Haganah) as did so many of my fellow students. Yet as an expression of my commitment to our society and to what was right for me, I remained a member of the Haganah (Jewish pre-state paramilitary underground organization), and decided to remain in Kibbutz Ginossar where my brother Immanuel was a member. This was a period that Erikson (1950) characterized as a moratorium—as stage in one's life when one could experiment with ideas, explore aspects of one's beliefs, and slowly "become" an autonomous individual. Thus, in retrospect, I understand that I used these years to groom myself for the future. While I worked in agriculture, I also worked in the library, got interested in the education of children and in the nature of living in an idealistic collective—the kibbutz. In time I, as an underground member of the Haganah, became a T.A.C. (Temporary Additional Constable) of the Coastal Watch which was in charge of guarding the coasts of Palestine, with the clandestine mission of enabling illegal immigrants, many of them survivors of the Holocaust, to illegally settle in Palestine. But then I also used some of my spare time to study for the London Matriculation, and later participated in a three-month-long and quite unusual seminar held by the Kibbutz Movement which was designed to prepare us for meeting (what are now referred to as) "Holocaust survivors".

I did not have clear expectations to live in a kibbutz and my stay there came to an end after four years. It ended one Sabbath towards the end of the World War when I went to visit my parents in Talpiot, on the outskirts of Jerusalem. As I was walking towards the downtown area of the city my eyes caught sight of the sign "British Council". I entered to inquire whether they had a stipend for studies in England, as studying there was an idea I had after passing my London Matriculation examination. I did so spontaneously out of the feeling that it was time to move on. When I told the receptionist there that I wanted to study English Literature, which had been my favorite subject in school, she said that to her regret they only had a stipend for "Colonial Social Science" at the London School of Economics and Political Science. I had no idea what this subject was all about, but I accepted the offer on the spot.

When this happened I delayed my return to the kibbutz for a few days. I submitted my application, was accepted to the program after having been interviewed first by three school inspectors and then by someone from the Jewish Agency, all of whom supported my application to study in London.

Three weeks later my parents took me to catch a taxi that took me to Lydda Airport for my flight via Cairo to London. As there was no connecting plane to London, for three weeks I roamed the unforgettable streets and museums of Cairo. I also stood at the zoo for hours observing the behavior of members of an orangutan family. The airline company paid my hotel bill while I waited for my flight to London. Finally in London, I took a taxi from Victoria Station to my relatives in Kensington, and I remember the driver saying after I had paid him, "thank you, sir" whereupon I responded, "thank you, sir". With hindsight, I remember that this interaction so clearly was not, I believe, as just chance, but a quest for connection. I believe that at that moment I must have been reminded of when I had arrived twelve years earlier, in Palestine, after having been excluded, nay expelled, from Nazi Germany. I am often reminded of the time after I succeeded in moving beyond my feeling of strangeness in the country which would eventually become our new home. That it became our home was enabled by both our caring family and its being a welcoming society. Having a home, I now believe, allowed me to move on to this next phase in London which did prepare me for my life's work.

And indeed, my experience in London shaped my life's work as a social worker, as I would say it today, as someone who conveys, sees his vocation and pursuit as a partner in enabling the "excluded in our midst" to move beyond exclusion and to acquire the capacity to connect. This I later named "reciprocity" as a connectedness in which each beneficiary is a benefactor.

Throughout my life connecting with others has repeatedly been my primary goal, both personally and professionally. To achieve this requires working to transform both the excluded themselves and the excluders: the former needing help in finding ways to belong and the latter needing to learn how to join the excluded and support them and himself in their search "to connect and reconnect". This quest, as set out in the rest of this book, to connect or reconnect is at the heart of both my professional pursuit as a social worker and as a citizen who has often been an outsider and who had learned—often with great effort—how to belong.

I am someone who at first thought that he wanted to become a student of literature and in the end became a social worker, one who came to consider social work to be all about what is encapsulated in the words of E.M. Forster's "Howard's End" (1910):

> Only connect! That was the whole of the sermon. Only connect the prose and the passion and both will be exalted, and human love will be seen at its height. Live in fragments no longer.

## 2. MOVING ON: TRAINING FOR SOCIAL WORK IN POST-WAR LONDON

While I never dreamt of nor aspired to becoming a social worker, I became one. And in doing so, I unwittingly followed Freud's suggestion not to allow anyone to give you advice on what profession or mate to choose. In retrospect, I realize that I followed his wisdom in both fields.

I remember landing in London at the beginning of 1946 expecting once again to feel like a safe outsider, which is how I and our Zionist family had felt after having left Germany. However, I "knew" it would end when the time came to move to Palestine. But then in Palestine, I often also felt as an outsider in a collective which was deliberately established to enable outsiders and newcomers like me to belong to it. As I now understand, these early experiences may have contributed to my becoming a social worker by raising my awareness that to be one, one had to be willing to be an outsider from within the mainstream, i.e. an outsider who would be ready to join others, the most excluded in our midst, to enable them to become a part of that collective. Social work was the only profession that made it its explicit double-mission to join the excluded and to accompany them on their journey beyond exclusion towards reciprocity (Rosenfeld, 1983).

Be that as it may, looking back after soon sixty years, I realize that, knowingly or not, I couldn't have made a better professional choice. Why? Because I now know that in few other professions could I have paved *my way* in such a worthwhile and challenging career that was never dull and never felt pointless. Of course I had heard about social workers before, even back in Germany, but the ones I knew had always seemed to me somewhat stern and not very tender. Later on, in Israel, I had the opportunity to meet many social workers of German origin with whom I was often in conflict when faced with their confrontational style and their reluctance to openly express their beliefs, rooted in German culture, where the children must be hardened in order to develop properly and not to succumb to tenderness, nay weakness.

Upon landing in London, I could not have known how well my "formative years" there would groom me for what was to come. I began my studies there at a turning point for the world: the war had just ended and in Palestine preparations were afoot for establishing the State of Israel. Coming to England provided me with an opportunity to prepare myself for serving later in the "State on the Way", the name by which Israel was known prior to statehood.

Pasteur's (1854) words that, "chance favors only the prepared mind", is a suitable phrase for explaining the extent to which my time in London paved the way for me, both professionally and personally. "Colonial Social Science" was an initiative of the Labor government at the end of the colonial period and designed to put into practice its vision of a Welfare State. Those of us who had come to study social work at that time were seen as privileged, if not ordained with a critical mission: to see the humanity of the needy back in our home countries. Our teachers, who had been evacuated to Cambridge because of air raids and subsequently alienated from active work with students throughout the years of the war, were thrilled to be back in London. For them, teaching us was both a challenge and an opportunity that they took on with great enthusiasm and even gratitude to us. I was exposed once again to high quality teachers, so this initial introduction to the social work profession left no room for regret but rather a feeling of immense gratitude, and produced an appealing sense of challenge that has remained with me ever since. This was, in no small part, also thanks to the unusual cohort of "colonial" students from Kenya, Yemen, Jamaica, Mauritius, which included the late Samy Geraisy, a Christian Arab from Kafar Kana, near Nazareth, the village in which Jesus had been born, Nechama Makower-Barzilai and David Reifen, all from Palestine. Indeed, I believe that all of us there were ever so thankful for the opportunities that these studies offered us.

I still remember my first day, when I entered a class on "social psychology" taught by Professor Maurice Ginsberg. I recall him saying something that I still grapple with today: "Sentiments are tender emotions". It is a statement that alerted me to an aspect of tenderness which until then no one had mentioned and which I do not remember learning or hearing about again in the course of my training there. Now I consider tenderness to be at the very heart of serving the "excluded in our midst"—those who have often been victims of violence and who especially are in need of our caring listening to their yearnings for tenderness, to being acknowledged for their humanity, for being like us. And as I later learned, it is this acknowledgement that is related to reciprocity, to the mutual recognition of the humanity of oneself and of the other.

Soon after this I met Professor Siegfried Nadel who proclaimed that we all had "action potential", referring to the positive element at the root of "changing the world" and which I think is at the heart of this book. On that same day he asked me to write an essay on "motivation for work in the kibbutz", a topic that was hardly ever discussed and certainly one I had never explored when I had lived on a kibbutz. In the kibbutz it was assumed that "motivation" was a critical but potentially explosive issue that was best left untouched so as not to criticize members of the kibbutz who did not live up to expectations. Indeed, the subject of motivation, which I was then writing about for the first time, has occupied my mind and work ever since. It is not easy to talk with others about what they have never thought about and that "not knowing" is not necessarily best left untouched. This is especially true that when criticizing somebody for lacking motivation, encourages him/her to continue shying away from change. After Professor Nadel had read what I wrote, he returned the paper to me without knowing how much I had struggled with writing it, and simply said with typical English understatement, "What you wrote is really quite good". This comment both moved and encouraged me for what was to come and even prepared me for it.

During my studies I also had my first exposure to the world of social work practice with families who had just returned from being evacuated from London, and with the children who had been placed in a palatial home that had previously been the residence of an aristocratic British family. The house, located in Fernhurst, Sussex, was called Ropes Hostel and it served as a rather un-inviting abode for homeless youth—a vast building not properly heated, and tended by people who treated the children entrusted to them in a highly impersonal manner, as if they were objects to be administered. I worked there with children and youth who felt totally lost after their houses had been bombed during the air attacks on London and their families split up. The challenge of working with these children and their families in a caring way became possible because I was supported by my highly qualified supervisors. I really did not know what to do at the beginning, but the experience I gained during this period gradually gave me the feeling that I could meet these challenges. One such experience was crucial in this respect. On one of my first days in this home, a boy of about eleven or twelve began what the staff saw as a "temper tantrum". Not knowing what to do, I simply walked up to him and hugged him. While everyone—the staff and the other children—were shocked, the boy very quickly leaned on me and calmed down. Perhaps it was the human touch that the hug represented or maybe it was simply that he felt that I cared for him. I am not sure. But this kind of on-the-spot intervention was very effective in that in its own small way it broke the patterns that had been established in the home. And if that were not enough, what also mattered was that we remained in touch and attached to each other.

After finishing my first round of studies as a colonial social worker in the making, I started to train as a mental health social worker. That I was able to pursue and to benefit from these studies was primarily made possible by our caring lecturers and by our dedicated supervisors in the field. What I learned from them was how to be deeply and humbly concerned about those with whom we were to work. I also learned to be deeply grateful for what our totally committed lecturers and highly competent field supervisors sought to impart to us. Let me explain. We students were from around the world, each in her or his particular way feeling alone and far from home. Our teachers in turn were always friendly, happy to meet us and open to addressing the particular concerns of each of us as human beings. For me this experience was especially intense as I was in a place outside of Palestine where I encountered next to no anti-Semitism. Their deep commitment both to the clients we served, whom they saw as people, and to us as students struggling to serve the clients, made that year totally unforgettable and inspiring. In fact, I now understand that our teachers facilitated a process by which we students partnered with them to create a rather unique learning community. Hence, as mentioned above, one of our teachers, Nadel, in assigning papers to us always tried to suggest topics which he, not only we, would learn from. The major lesson I learned there concerns social work and its twin missions of providing resources for people in need and allowing the creation of primary groups marked by strong connections and mutual support.

After completing my studies, while still in London, I was asked to join the medical corps of the new Israeli Army as a military mental health worker. I clearly recall how shortly prior to returning to the newly-established State of Israel, I went to have my last meeting with my tutor, Mrs. Kay MacDougall. While I had just come to thank her and say goodbye, she asked me, in her ever-so-straightforward manner: "Why do you look so worried?" I explained that I was destined to serve in the Israeli Army. She persisted and asked again, "So, why are you so worried?" I told her that I would have to serve as a psychiatric social worker with no experience in this field. She continued, "But why are you so worried after having done so well in your studies?" I answered that I would have to work in a demanding job in the army and felt that I had little knowledge and especially lacked intuition for doing this work. Thereupon she told me something unforgettable: "Don't worry, intuition is a matter of experience."

This kind of guiding encouragement is something that has accompanied me ever since, in many situations throughout my career. Repeatedly resorting to the definition of intuition being a matter of experience eventually led me, several decades later, to suggest that the "craft" of social work is "the invention of interventions" (Rosenfeld, 1983), which obviously had to do with my relying on experience. I dared to write this since inventing requires a readiness to use intuition rather than to work in the standard manner of applying theories and following methodologies that were the fashion of the day. This point is related to what I consider the social worker's primary commitment: to serve those I have come to call the "un(der) served in our midst". It turned out that such service—aided by my "intuition"—also made me feel safe and well enough equipped to become a social activist. By this I mean that I see activism not as an attack on existing institutions but rather as a constant effort at mobilizing help for the underserved. In fact, it seems to me that social work is suited only for those who dare to engage in work with and on behalf of persons with multiple and diverse needs.

Hence I believe that social work is not a profession that should train specialists but rather demands a readiness to be constantly willing to face multiple challenges, many of which are forbidding and at times may be seen as rather outlandish. Along these lines, I came to see the basis of social work as creating partnerships—"joint ventures" in more contemporary parlance—and that because of this we can understand that the profession calls for owning and living up to the tender emotions, and the recognition of the humanity of others. At the time I sensed it, but I now know that tender emotions are at the heart of social work, and at the heart of any kind of partnership for social change, as an invitation for tenderness.

With that in mind, and while facing these challenges, I have scarcely ever felt overwhelmed or lost. I attribute this, to a large extent, to the fact that I have always been able to connect to a number of caring and responsive "co-leagues" in the same "league" who were ready to explore what needed to be done and then to persevere in our work. These were the kinds of "co-leagues" who acted as partners to others even while not truly knowing what the other needed. To bestow on them just this kind of caring could only come about when, as I had mentioned before, there was a belief in and a dedication, to that which the excluded in our midst so clearly lacked—namely, tenderness. By tenderness—that unspoken art of social work—I refer to the ability to talk about and expose our difficulties, how highly personal they may be and to do so in ways that confronting them leads to attempts to solve them rather than to putting them aside. The best of partners were those who cared for others often without clearly knowing what the others really needed, whether they were ready or not to be both their benefactors and their beneficiaries. It were those who cared in a way that did not revert into a cold, distant or estranged attitude and readily stayed engaged with the underserved. Certainly, it is difficult to convey the special circumstances in which we lived after the Second World War and within which I was taking my first professional steps. The period during which I learned to be a social worker was a time in which the world was devastated, millions were displaced and in many places only rudimentary services were being rebuilt very slowly. It is against this background that we encountered the survivors of the Holocaust who were often seen as the dregs of humanity and we had to learn not to just support them but to actively help them to confront what they had gone through.

These formative years were a kind of "grande finale", foreshadowing a "daring" social worker who "does not want to explain the world but to change it"[1]. This idea, which I heard years later from Chris Argyris, is also a guiding idea of this book and of my life's work.

I will end this section by saying how these rich years both preceded and prepared me for my career as a social worker. They enabled me to be a social worker who is enough of an outsider to pave his own way, and enough of an insider, to do so for the benefit of those clients whom the core of society often sees as outsiders. And to do both—to be loyal and at the same time an outsider—can best be done by someone who feels comfortable meeting the challenges of this ever-changing world.

## 3. MY FIRST ASSIGNMENT: WHEN THE ARMY IS A PLACE FOR MORE THAN JUST WAGING WAR

In September 1948 I landed back in what had previously been Palestine and was now Israel and which at that time was in the midst of its War of Independence. This landing was quite different than the one I had had fifteen years earlier in Haifa. Then, I had arrived as an immigrant with my mother on a luxurious ship and now I came as a budding social worker on an unsafe airplane from London. This time I arrived in the middle of the night in full darkness (because of the blackout) into a country at war and with no one to meet me. If that were not enough, upon my arrival I was immediately transferred to a Military Transit Camp. It took me two days to persuade an officious and suspicious officer that I should not be sent to a basic training camp but rather be issued an army number and assigned to the military psychiatric unit in the north of the country. What ultimately convinced the officer was the copy I showed him of a psychological test that had been used by the British Army.

Ours was the first psychiatric unit set up in the army. It was formed by a group of foreigners—yes, outsiders—most of whom had come or, like me, returned from abroad to join the army. Our base of operations was an army hospital in Haifa. Some of us came specifically to treat soldiers suffering from "shell shock" or post-traumatic stress disorder, and that was, at least initially, the primary reason for the existence of the unit. However, it became a very isolated unit because, for whatever reason, few soldiers with primary battle trauma were referred to us. Some of the soldiers referred were those whom the army wanted to discharge and not surprisingly many were both new immigrants and recent survivors of the war and the persecution in Europe. While only a few of them had been soldiers in World War II, some of them did have a lot to tell about their recent devastating experiences on the battlefields of Israel. Unable to talk about their past, they were also blocked from preparing themselves for a future because trauma—leading one to be constantly "living" in the past—does not easily allow one to live in the present and create the tools needed for the future.

Menachem was one of the first soldiers assigned to me and the first Holocaust survivor whom I got to know well. He had participated in a battle in the Galilee hills where a soldier next to him was killed. In the aftermath of this event Menachem was considered as "post-traumatic". After he had failed to respond to psychiatric treatment due to his complete preoccupation with the past, I was entrusted with the task of helping him with his rehabilitation, in anticipation of his pending release from the army.

The minute Menachem entered the room he showed me his sweaty hands and said that the sweating had started during the battle on the mountains of the Galilee. All that I could do then and there was to listen to him. As he recounted his recent arrival from Poland, I immediately observed his sense of total helplessness and defeat and heard that he was completely alone with no one he knew around him. As to myself, I was too overwhelmed to dare to ask him any details about his home, his wartime experiences, his family, or about his life during the war in Europe. All I could do was to be attuned to what was uppermost in his mind: his feeling of having been very insensitively treated by those who were meant to "rehabilitate" him. Their attempts to help were futile and utterly meaningless to him and, indeed, to those workers themselves as well, since they did not confront, did not know how to confront, his sorrow and loneliness. At that time, the efforts of people charged with the "rehabilitation" of Holocaust survivors were focused not on their feelings but solely on "action items", on impelling them to seek work or education, to "do" something with their lives. This attitude, while prompted by well-meaning policies, resulted in highly impersonal interactions with people who had come from Europe.

As a novice, all I could do was to accompany Menachem to his rehabilitation worker, and tell him a bit about this survivor about whom I myself knew very little. This took place while the country was still in the middle of the war and when the rehabilitation workers employed by the government were themselves totally overwhelmed and did not really know what they were supposed to do. So, to stop this official from behaving in a cold and unfeeling manner I spoke with him about Menachem as if I were the rehabilitation officer, even though neither of us knew too much about rehabilitation. From time to time I saw Menachem again and whenever we met he showed me his sweating hands. I looked at them seriously without saying a word. Not knowing what else I could do, I repeatedly asked him—one of my first ad-hoc inventions—to tell me about the soldier who had died next to him in battle.

Only later did I understand that asking just this simple question was what addressing past traumas was all about.

What strikes me in hindsight is that Menachem, who felt so helpless, was treated by rehabilitation workers, including myself as a member of the psychiatric unit, who felt equally helpless vis-à-vis this work, which was entirely new for all of us. The last time I saw Menachem was when he told me that he was trying to become a carpenter. There he was, the same heavily-built, somewhat dead-looking fellow, whose unrequited helplessness I remember to this day.

What I learned from this period is that however fragile our base of operations may be, it challenges us to learn how to treat people who themselves have so little ground under their feet. For many people, military service, as an in-between period, provided an opportunity to use the army as a means to forge a collective path, to "graduate" into our common, new and evolving society. It also allowed people to undergo an individual process of preparation and transformation for what was to come: the establishment of the state of Israel and its new society. Today it may be hard to understand how in the late 1940s and the early 1950s I, like many of my contemporaries, was so deeply committed to establishing a Jewish homeland, partly out of our active commitment to the newcomers to the country.

Fortunately, after seventeen months of service, I was appointed to the reserve corps as a psychiatric social worker, later as a mental health officer. I was to take part in establishing a post-war military mental health service that was so essential for Israel's new army. I served in this role as part of my reserve duty, once a month for around twenty-five years, and full time during three separate wars. On the basis of these experiences my colleagues and I formulated an approach for facilitating the integration of ill-equipped recruits into the army, by challenging and countering their sense of exclusion. The approach which emerged was designed to help all of us, professionals and soldiers alike, to contribute to both our own well-being and to that of the surrounding society. The actual modes of working are described more fully in my article entitled "Serving the Individual and the Collective: Lessons from the Wars of Israel" (Rosenfeld, 1980). In that article one of my contentions was that for many, if not most Holocaust survivors, the expectation that they can and will serve the state instead of being considered "cripples" did in itself carry the message about how worthy they were to their new collective and that to serve indeed meant to belong. These experiences also inspired me to carry out and then write an unpublished comparative study together with Yehuda Matras, a sociologist and demographer I had met in Chicago (Rosenfeld and Matras, 1989). We showed that the social mobility of young men and women from diverse backgrounds who had each experienced exclusion[2] —especially as new immigrants—had benefited enormously from their army service.

Another significant lesson from that period, one which has continued to serve me and many others today, is related to my work with Holocaust survivors. My colleagues and I learned to listen to the unbearable stories the survivors shared with us at a time when the general tendency was, at all costs, "to overcome" the experience of the Holocaust and avoid looking back. What enabled me and others to face these stories, and encourage others to do so, was the conviction that however terrible the past had been "the future can only be built on the real past", as stated in a poignant T.S. Eliot quotation that I once heard. This lesson, that listening and hearing about the past is a powerful tool for healing and for building a worthwhile future, has stayed with me. This is reflected, for instance, in the story of Chaim (section V2), in my first published article, "A Mother whose Child would not Eat" (Rosenfeld and Brandt, 1956) (to which I shall presently turn) and in my work on "Learning from Success" (section IV).

What is common to these cases is the idea of "unlinking" harsh realities in the present from the horrors of the past. A separation is made possible both by daring to refer to what has been in the past and to juxtapose it with what is in the present. This distinguishes the "here and now" from the "then and there" and thus lets it go and frees one to move on. In hindsight, I believe that, in contrast to the care provided by physicians, who saw mainly symptoms and not people, one of the things that enabled Holocaust survivors to move beyond the horrors of their past was connecting with us, their caregivers, since we were among the very few who actually talked to them about their past. It was this kind of connection that I had learned to make and which required us to be present and available to support them in whatever here and now they found themselves. Correspondingly, this connection also enabled their communities, despite their shortcomings, to be there for them as they left the oppressive past behind on their way to a freer present. In some way this was a forerunner of my later conscious commitment to initiating "reciprocity" to the excluded in our midst.

## 4. WELL-BABY CENTERS IN JERUSALEM: BEING THERE AT THE BEGINNINGS

When I was released from the Army in early 1950, it was my good fortune to begin working as a social worker at the well-endowed and pioneering Lasker Mental Health and Child Guidance Clinic of the American-based Hadassah Medical Organization in Jerusalem.

The Clinic was directed by the late Dr. Gerald Caplan, with whom I had studied in London and worked with before in the Israeli Army. Dr. Caplan was a daring innovator in the fields of infant and child mental health. He was someone who held beginnings and innovations in great esteem and I, then a budding social worker, benefited enormously from his vision and wisdom. Specifically, I refer to the fact that Dr. Caplan saw the system of Well-Baby Centers as a universal service catering to all of Israel's population regardless of their income, place of residence or ethnic group. No less important at that time, in contrast to the prevailing medical view of children's caretaking that focused on symptoms and their treatment, he was interested in maternity and in parents.

One day I entered a Well-Baby Center[3] in Machane Yehuda, an outdoor fresh fruit and vegetable market in the heart of Jerusalem, which I knew only as a place to buy provisions and since our home-help had lived there. I, a total newcomer to these centers, had to introduce the staff of nurses there to Dr. Caplan's approach which was entirely new and foreign to these caregivers. We asked them to "work" with and for the benefit of mothers who had difficulties with their infants, to initiate care with all pregnant women and to engage other professionals, including social workers and nurses, to do all they could to enable young mothers and fathers to find their parental voices.

It is hard to imagine how new and challenging this was for me, particularly as a male social worker.

My first "client" there was the unforgettable Holocaust survivor, Mrs. Mizrachi, who had married a greengrocer from Kurdistan immediately after spending three solitary years at a religious boarding school for girls in Jerusalem. Mrs. Mizrachi entered my room at the Center with both arms outstretched at a maximum distance from her body holding her two-month-old daughter and saying mournfully, "you see, she doesn't eat and she isn't gaining any weight". Fortunately, thanks to the supervision I had received at the time from Dr. Margaret Brandt, a pediatrician and a psychoanalyst, I dared to engage Mrs. Mizrachi in a conversation about her background. In our talk, she referred to herself as the sole survivor of her family, all of whom had perished in a concentration camp in Europe. She spoke directly and with rather detached effect about how years before, while in the concentration camp, she had stolen food which had belonged to her aunt. With the apparent guilt for having taken the food, she hinted that she blamed herself for her aunt's death. On her next visit, I served as a kind of "sounding board" for Mrs. Mizrachi's thoughts and also gently mentioned to her that her aunt's name sounded quite similar to that of her daughter. All I could do was to listen to her and to repeatedly point out the similarity in the two names. After five or six meetings, to my great surprise Mrs. Mizrachi's daughter had started to gain weight. I assumed that it was because she had been freed from seeing her newborn daughter as a monument for the aunt who, she believed, had died because of her having stolen her food.

Mrs. Mizrachi was the first mother I had ever been asked to work with and the first mother I had ever met who had survived the Holocaust. My interaction with her left me with a good feeling about my capacity to be her partner in helping pave her way for herself and her baby at the beginning of their shared life. As I would say today, Mrs. Mizrachi and her daughter were among the first people with whom I set the stage for "moving beyond exclusion".

A few weeks later I visited the home of a woman who, soon after the Israeli War of Independence, had given birth to a boy she called "Yigal", meaning "he who will save". I later learned Yigal was a very popular name, intentionally given to boys in post-war Israel, where to be saved was uppermost in people's minds. Being a mother suffering from post-partum depression, she had refused to come to the Well-Baby Center and so I decided to visit her home. After opening the door while holding Yigal in her arms, she asked me to sit down and showed me how the screaming Yigal refused to take a bottle of milk that she was forcing into his mouth. Quite intuitively, I saw her forceful attempt to insert the bottle into the baby's mouth as a violent attack with sexual overtones. It reminded me of theories I had learned about in the past. What she was doing was like pushing a penis into a baby's mouth. Be that as it may, upon seeing this, I had the good sense to say to her, "I could never give birth to a child." I said so hoping to suggest to her that she, as a woman, was capable of the gentleness of women, and that hence she could succeed as a mother. Whatever this spontaneous intervention might have meant, Yigal's mother burst into unexplained laughter, put the bottle aside and simply embraced Yigal, who stopped crying. I never saw her again but as the nurse told me later, this mother had started coming to the center and was breast- feeding Yigal without a bottle.

For me this is an unforgettable example of an unrehearsed and innovative intervention. It was one which did not seem to be miraculous because I was able to relate it to what psychoanalysts called "penis envy".

On the face of it, the importance of these two stories is that they confirm the value of making use of known theories to facilitate change in people in the context of an ordinary center for mothers and babies. In the first story I relied on the powerful connection between the new-born child and the deceased aunt. It was a story about a mother who had survived the Holocaust and who had difficulties in nursing her first born. This came to an end and her motherhood took over when we together realized that her daughter had been named after her aunt whose food the mother had taken and who had eventually died. In the second story, my intervention served to free the mother from being stuck in evoking sentiments relating to male aggression around first born boys. Each mother was freed from her own unconscious fantasies which were barring her to be a tender mother at the start of her child's life. These experiences, especially in the aftermath of both the Holocaust and Israel's War of Independence, alerted me to the unique opportunities which these Well-Baby Centers offered parents to be "good enough", even after all they had experienced.

Consciously or not, I began to connect each story to the next, in a cumulative manner, and that became one beginning of my interest in learning from success. What it taught me was not to be imprisoned in on theory-based interventions as the source of practice, but that one has to be ready to learn in the course of identifying the actions employed is especially essential in new situations, as at the "beginning of life".

The importance of this kind of approach became clear to me in a different way when, later on, I learned from ATD Fourth World Movement that "only the best is good enough" for people living in extreme poverty, for whom high quality services, although critical, were commonly inaccessible. At the same time, offering high quality services is particularly important for the most socially excluded families who are not well-resourced and who are served by poorly equipped universal services. Hence, since Well-Baby Centers also provided innovative services to pregnant women, many of whom felt safe enough to share with their nurses their fantasies and desires, including nightmares related to pregnancies and unborn children. It seemed particularly important to reflect openly with these mothers on their emotions because they were mothers who were living in exclusion and who had few resources available to talk about themselves and how to work through lingering pain from their past. Over time, increasing numbers of pregnant women began to participate in the group meetings initiated at the centers, and which eventually became part of the work of more and more Well-Baby Centers around the country.

In reviewing the five years I spent there, I have come to believe that there was a parallel process that occurred in the Centers: as nurses assumed more and more professional autonomy, mothers became more and more able to "claim" their own motherhood. In that vein, I shall mention two examples of how nurses became what I would today call "Learning Companions"[4] to women at the beginnings of their motherhood. These examples show how, as the nurses dared to find their own voices rather than just serving as conduits for the instructions of pediatricians, they became ready and more capable of becoming true caregivers (Rosenfeld and Levy, 1997) in the spirit of what has since been named "the science of caring" (Watson, 1979). In line with my ongoing work with these nurses, I have learned how important it is to accompany mothers who have difficulties on their "journeys" towards parenthood and how this is bound to have an impact on launching the next generations of children. Moreover, even as other prenatal and early-childhood services have decreased over the years, Well-Baby Centers have remained in operation and are appreciated both by the professional community and by the families themselves.

The first example is of a stout and sturdy mother from Kurdistan who stalked in with two children leaning on her long dress and with a newborn in her arms. At the conclusion of their meeting I heard the nurse tell the mother, "so, now remember, that you must nurse the baby every four hours, that you have to clean your breasts and that you have to sit in a quiet and separate room". Thereupon both the mother and the nurse nodded their heads. After the mother had gone, the nurse said to me: "I know, and I know that she knows, that I told her that because that is what the pediatricians expect me to say".

The second example is when, after two years of work in this center, I dared to support the nurses when they chose to close down a special kitchen that quite harshly directed mothers on how to feed their babies. I mention both of these events because they illustrate how in those years it was essential to help nurses in Well-Baby Centers practice their craft of accompanying these mothers as partners, rather than act as mouthpieces for physicians who, at that time, still saw nurses as their orderlies.

In retrospect, on the basis of these two examples, I would say that after five years of work in these centers, nurses started to find their own voices and thus becoming what I have referred to as "learning companions" to the mothers. In creating reciprocal relations with the mothers, the nurses enabled these mothers to become self-directed learners in the course of their parenting.

Finally, two further developments from this period strongly affected my future work in the center. The first was my better understanding and recognition of the power of preventive programs. I saw how promoting the development of high quality services at the beginning of life, rather than waiting until acute crises develop in children later on, made increasingly good sense and resulted in engaging in ongoing development. The second relates to my growing recognition that the provision of appropriate parent-child services was critical enough to justify my deep investment throughout my career in work with nurses at these centers and my later political struggles to prevent the centers from closing down or moving towards privatization.

Some forty years later, upon my retirement from the university, when I returned to work with Well-Baby Center nurses, I introduced an approach I called "To Be a 'Good Enough' Parent", which has by now become standard practice in many of these centers. It is an approach based on steering away from a constant preoccupation with some kind of impossible quest to be the "perfect" parent, and towards a perspective that is based on utilizing the resources at the disposal of the mothers and fathers.

## NOTES

1. A statement I had heard from Chris Argyris when I met him at Harvard University in the 1990s. This is reminiscent of what Karl Marx had written in 1845 in a pamphlet entitled "Thesis on Feuerbach", first published after his death in 1888: *"'Philosophers have hitherto only interpreted the world in various ways; the point is to change it"*. This latter is engraved at the entrance to Humbolt University in Berlin.

2. There we showed that these young men had grown up in disenfranchised families and then joined a youth movement and/or served in the Army.

3. Well-Baby Centers, which were established in Palestine in 1922, are a much-appreciated universal country-wide service for parents and their infants and children during pregnancy and until the age of 6. The nurses who are the mainstay of these centers are also expected to provide services which are appropriate for families-at-risk. In that tradition, we introduced an ongoing training program for nurses named "To be a Good Enough Parent" with a special focus on providing families-at-risk with the help which was required to be "good enough" (See section IV.6).

4. See Part V on Learning Companions.

*III*

# Six Years in Chicago: "Unleashing Hidden Potential"* on Learning the Craft of Social Work

INTRODUCTION: LEARNING THE CRAFT OF SOCIAL WORK
FROM THE PAST AND FOR THE FUTURE

After years of becoming a social worker in the newly established State of Israel, I sensed that it was time to move on. To do so I asked my employers, the Hadassah Medical Organization of America in Israel, whose first social worker in Israel I had been, to sponsor my application for a stipend to study for a Ph.D. at the School of Social Service Administration at the University of Chicago. There I was to spend more than six years for studying and learning more about the for me so challenging engagement in the profession of social work into which I had slipped luckily and unknowingly, and where I had felt so relevant: first as a mental health social worker in the army; then as a member of the Lasker Mental Health and Child Guidance Clinic of Hadassah in Jerusalem, where I had worked in Well-Baby Clinics as well as in Youth Aliyah—an organization for mainly immigrant children and youth from the Holocaust, and also with families in Jerusalem. These were also years when I tried to find my own ways as a professional social worker under conditions which could not have been any better.

Yes, and all that after my earlier studies at the London School of Economics, and after I had received a BA in sociology and education at the Hebrew University in Jerusalem. All that came to an end when, after seven years in

Jerusalem, I felt that the time was ripe for going on to devote myself fully to being a full time student and as it turned out for six years in which I groomed myself for the future.

On my way to Chicago, I spent a few months in London which was familiar and where I had friends with whom I could stay. There I also made contact with different human service institutions. For instance, I participated together with Elisabeth Bott and Eric Trist of the Tavistock Institute of Human Relations in a one-time marketing study on how to introduce soft tissue toilet paper in England. There I also had the opportunity to sit in at meetings with Anna Freud and Melanie Klein two doyens of psychoanalysis. All this made me aware of how much there was to which I could aspire. If that were not enough, I was also invited to become an assistant to Professor Richard Titmuss of the London School of Economics, one of the founding fathers of the Welfare State. But then I dared to turn this offer down when my sociology teacher and friend from Jerusalem, Shmuel Eisenstadt, suggested that I move to Chicago because I had already come to know London and was ripe for getting to know another society, that this was the right choice. I was further convinced of this after having read with fascination J.D. Salinger's "The Catcher in the Rye" (Salinger, 1951). It is a novel that deals with the lives of the young generation of Americans which allowed them to have their own opinions, something that strengthened my sense that I should take the opportunity of studying in the United States.

Thus boarding the ship from London to New York seemed to have been an attempt to maximize the "years of wandering", and enter the years of "wondering" to come. With this carefree frame of mind I entered my six years of life in Chicago, the life of a "learner", no longer an "apprentice", one eager to be taught and not yet a "master" ready to teach. Looking back, I find that I could not have "chosen" a better venue for doing just that.

I arrived in Chicago on a Friday and initially stayed in an alienating and lonely Y.M.C.A. near the university. The only person I knew in Chicago was my late friend Jehoshua Ramot, a psychiatrist with whom I had previously shared an apartment in London, and who left Chicago to work in New York the day after my arrival. Fortunately his wife Bracha, a very special person and also a physician, was there and she and I spent my first Saturday evening together at the home of Ruth and Elihu Katz, both from the University of Chicago and later the Hebrew University of Jerusalem. There I met Ezra Levin, who became a close friend and who, like me, was looking for an apartment. Right then and there we agreed to rent an apartment knowing that with Ezra, we would have a kosher kitchen. This we did for a whole year living together, and became the beginning of a life-long friendship.

This home base had also made it possible to connect with the few Israeli friends I had made upon arriving there and enabled me to ready myself for the learning ahead. While feeling like an outsider I knew that I was fortunate not to have any financial worries, neither personal nor national ones and the first time free for learning.

Beyond this and because of where I had come from, soon after my arrival I found on one of the walls a slogan which accompanied me all the years there. It said: "It could not be done, it could not be done, we did it." In hindsight, this seems to have summed up important elements from both where I had come from and, unknowingly, for the years of becoming where I had arrived. It gave expression to upholding my desires for what would be where I had arrived: to engage in challenging, if not adventurous, opportunities and undertakings and to do so with determination, to engage in finding inventive solutions for the intellectual and professional challenges I could engage in, in that so liberal and liberating University of Chicago and its School of Social Work (Social Service Administration).

## 1. ON BECOMING THE SOCIAL WORKER I BECAME AT THE SCHOOL OF SOCIAL SERVICE ADMINISTRATION IN CHICAGO

When I came to the university I had no clear idea as to what I wanted to study and learn, and no one there asked me. Thus, without any introduction, I simply started with the prescribed courses and, reacted to most of them somewhat superciliously.

Only in hindsight can I say that I could not have found a better setting for studying and learning which enabled me to pave my own way and not as in the past, paved those of others. By not knowing that the former is possible and expected, I reacted quite critically to the required courses, always with the sense of "I know it" and flunked the first year exams.

In the same vein, I presented the first findings of a study on continuers and continues in a psychiatric therapy in which I participated, with the staff of the hospital (Rosenfeld and Orlinsky, 1961). I did so by unknowingly degrading psychologists—who had been poor in predicting who would be continuers of the psychotherapy that had been offered. At that time no one of the staff present intervened and only later I understood that they were at best puzzled.

But no one of the staff and any other openly intervened and let me, a relatively experienced social worker, find my way. It was this tolerance and trust of the staff of the school which enabled me to choose my own topic for my PhD research which was in many ways not in line with the modes of practice and research methodologies of the school. While they sought how to win over non-continuers for the service offered I, learning from the latter, sought out how the non-continuing patients had been helped in the past as a source of knowledge for how to serve them in the present. This being once again an unbeknownst precursor of "learning from success", i.e. learning from the successes of the past, rather than following the ideas of professionals.

What made all this possible was that I had come to a university and a professional school which was committed to enabling their students to be or become independent learners, and not as appliers of prevailing knowledge and theories. In retrospect, that meant that I was encouraged to follow my own quest for learning, i.e. what I craved for and believed in and not a follower.

This is what made the freedom I had to study what I had in mind, with regard to social work and beyond it, which really gave me the chance and necessity to engage in "ongoing Learning" which, in time, became one of my most liberating ideas and pursuits. It was all this that had enabled me to pave my own way and to follow that I considered as relevant to the mission of social work. It was this freedom which allowed or enabled me to pursue what I have described in this book, and about all my commitment to "serving the un(der) served in our midst" and to do so with the ensuing commitment to "learning from success". Indeed, it was that mode of learning which has inspired and guided me as a teacher, and researcher of social work ever since. Indeed, it is this freedom to "invent" new ways rather than to "follow" the prevailing ways of social work. In retrospect, I understood that this suited the professional pursuit of social work in this ever changing world which requires one to be open to the varieties of knowledge for practice. It is this which, in hindsight, had encouraged Krumer Nevo (2000) declare that what is required is knowledge from the field, from practice rather than from "academia". But it was in the academia of Chicago where I had been exposed to so many learning opportunities that I owe to them the widening of multiple sources of learning for social work that had guided my engagement in this profession and the ways of practicing it ever since.

## 2. TO BE A SOCIAL WORKER ONE NEEDS TO OVERCOME THE "STRANGENESS BETWEEN HELPER AND CLIENT"[1]

As I have mentioned, I had not chosen to be a social worker but, as Freud said, I "then slipped quickly and easily into it" (Freud, 1900, page 397). From early on I thought that the task of a social worker was to serve "the most excluded in our midst", although to do so was not very prestigious and not all of those around me were impressed by my choice. I became aware of this when, during my early studies in Chicago, I learned that kindergarten teachers were looked down upon because of the low prestige of the children, and, that similarly, the prestige of social work was low because of the low prestige of its "clients". Like kindergarten teachers, they were not respected even for what the latter did or did not do for young children, even though that was crucial for the latter's futures. Indeed, they were not as respected as university professors who, because the university students they taught, gave them high social status. Later on, this insight inspired me to tell my students of social work that once they believe it possible, they could benefit from their "clients" and learn from them differently but no less if not more than university professors could learn from their students.

Accordingly, I was always fascinated by two phenomena. The first was how much I, as a social worker, benefited from what "clients" had to contribute. For instance, it is incredible how much I learned about the Holocaust, about which I knew almost nothing before serving some of its survivors, as a Mental Health Officer in the Israeli army. Another example is what I had learned from my teacher John Bowlby (Bowlby, 1969) during my training at the Tavistock Clinic in London. During the "Blitz" he was studying how the separation of children from their mother had a devastating effect on their capacity for attachment. This was also the first time I discovered that infants have something to contribute to their mothers, and is, I believe, in tune with what Donald Winnicott (Winnicott, 1953) implied when he wrote about being a "good enough mother".

The second was my deep interest in figuring out who the social workers were whose clients remained in treatment but who rarely received the acknowledgement they deserved for their crafts and their efforts. Based on my experience, I had to deeply admire their capacity to serve the least well-equipped patients and clients whom others had not been able to serve. These after all were "the excluded in our midst", those whom I came to consider to be the primary beneficiaries of social work. All this is what had led me to focus my study on discovering the nature of their quest for help rather than to adjust to what their helpers expected from them or what they assumed the clients desired. To follow these assumptions were forerunners of "learning from success".

Thus, at this point, and thanks to the very caring staff of the School of Social Service Administration, I set out on my way. I could take any course I wanted and in any department of the University of Chicago. I was free to dream up the topic of my PhD thesis which was approved by members of my PhD committee and which both they and I only in time came to fully understand. This unexpected trust in my becoming did not happen by chance at the University of Chicago. It was there that one called the professors by their first names, where there was a minimal number of prerequisite courses, and where I could choose and find those courses, those teachers and those topics I considered to be most useful, and most of which, as it also turned out, became very relevant.

Among the staff of the School of Social Service Administration, I am especially grateful to the members of my PhD Committee, Professors Mary McDonald, Helene Perlman and Margaret Ripple, who were supportive during the four years I needed to find, by myself, my own way with my thesis. At the University of Chicago, I learned much from Edward Shills, for instance, about the differences between "primary and secondary relationships". The former, "primary", were with a minimum of rules, like in sexual intercourse, and the latter, "secondary", were dominated by rules, like the cells of a Communist Party.

At the University of Chicago the professor of sociology Everett Hughes taught us about various professions and amongst them he mentioned "ambulance chasers". These were lawyers who, on their way to the hospital, made injured people sign that they, the lawyers, would receive 50% of the compensation which, thanks to them, the injured parties may receive from insurance companies. However distasteful this was, it helped me to understand that one can invent, nay shape, one's profession in ways that one considered appropriate. This made me dare to think that social work could be a profession with a calling and that could preserve the dignity which I believed it deserved.

I also studied with Bruno Bettelheim, the psychoanalyst and founder of the Orthogenic School in Chicago. I cannot forget that one of his staff members told me that he had once been harsh to a child suffering from autism, telling him that, "I get harsh in order to help you not to be willing to do something so drastic". What I also will never forget is Bettelheim's work, on "Individual and Mass Behavior in Extreme Situations" (Bettelheim, 1943) in which he writes about the people he was with during the late thirties in the concentration camps of Dachau and Buchenwald. He discovered that those who survived the camp were autonomous persons with deep beliefs, religious or any other. That was one of the first times in my life that I became more aware of there being successes, successes which could easily have been predicted and which, unexpectedly, were brought about by on reciprocity-based insights and studies. At that time I was just puzzled by this unexpected finding, but in time it led me to focus on "positive deviances"—that is, successful behaviors enabling individuals to find better solutions to problems they face—as a point of departure for what was to become the basis for learning from success.

There were many others there from whom I chose to learn, and this and much else convinced me that at this university I had the time and was in a place where I could choose a topic for my thesis without anyone telling me how I was to conduct my study. The unassuming ways in which members of my committee accompanied me enabled me to prepare myself for what would be my future work. I consider this to have become a "turning point" on my way to achieving my own autonomy. I did this without having to search for the approval of anybody else. I learned that generosity, as well as tolerance of differences, rather than control and coercion with their focus on teaching or instruction, were what created the opportunities for exploring the unknown.

This idea itself had been put into words in the early fifties in Jerusalem where my very special friend and social worker, who was at that time my highly valued supervisor Pauline Miller-Shereshefsky, introduced me to the ideas of Otto Rank which lay at the basis of the "functional school of social work" (Taft, 1944). The idea of this "school" of social work, in contrast to the prevalent "diagnostic" one (basically problem-solving on the basis of indicators of symptoms), supported me in my need of not just "doing it my way" or in the ways of the client, but by the way of its being functional, i.e. by the way in which it would be of the most benefit to those involved. At that time, unknowingly, I became able to do and to convey what needed to be done in contrast to researchers who were caught up in rejecting and confirming available hypotheses rather than discovering alternatives that also took into account the "will" of the one who needs the provision of help. I remember a story that encapsulates this idea. Mr. Marx comes into an agency. There he asked for a pair of shoes, whereupon the social worker asked him, "To wear or to stand in?" All this was based on Rank's idea (1947) that psychotherapy existed to enable each to discover his "will", i.e. to own that capacity over which he had or could have control, and which furthered his freedom and autonomy. About this possibility and the right to make choices, I also learned from a renowned pianist who said the following in regard to how one should play a piece of music: Not as the one who played the piece would or as one presumed that the composer would have wanted it but as the piece of music wanted to be played.[2]

The idea of using one's autonomy to groom oneself for the future enabled me, later on, to accept seeing myself as a stranger or an outsider as an opportunity for becoming a social worker who does not feel superior to the people served and one who is not pre-occupied with his place in the social hierarchy. This was for me a beginning which I was later able to continue, but not before I had discovered the ATD Fourth World Movement; a movement addressing the needs of families living in extreme poverty and exclusion. They do so by addressing all three parties whom I consider to be partners in the work of social work: those who have the resources, those who need them and social workers or others who contribute to the transactions between the first two. In time, I saw this to be the heart of social work—seeing all three as partners in creating the kind of reciprocity which the move beyond exclusion requires.

It is this partnership to which I shall turn now.

## 3. TO SERVE THE EXCLUDED IN OUR MIDST REQUIRES THE "INVENTION OF INTERVENTIONS"

Over time I came to realize that often social workers would fault their clients for needing help in the first place; for lacking the "motivation" or "capacity" to use the "help" they were offered and even for failing to change. In contrast to this idea, I came to see social workers as helpers who were there to "invent interventions" in order to find solutions for change based on knowing and understanding who their clients are (Rosenfeld, 1983). With that in mind and thanks to my studies in anthropology, it dawned on me that it was up to us social workers to learn with and from anyone who needs help. This shift in the mindset would eventually enable the profession to discover ways of acting which, without necessarily basing itself on explanations, would bring about change[3].

I began to understand that such change would depend on the reversal of the exclusion of our "clients" and then on our connecting and accompanying them towards what I later came to refer to as reciprocity. It was when facing the excluded in our midst that I recognized that it was up to us, as social workers, to initiate seeking them out and putting into words what was necessary for building bridges beyond exclusion. With this in mind, I began from then on to call myself and others involved in this kind of learning to be "learning companions"[4], who are at the disposal of those needing partners to engage in joint learning to shift us and them towards finding roads beyond exclusion. In all realms of exclusion this approach, including work in the area of mental health in which at that time I had the most experience, became a basis for my actively and deliberately seeking ways to join those who required help and to become partners in their efforts to move beyond exclusion (Rosenfeld, 1993).

In the sequence of this understanding, the highlight of my years in Chicago was, when in about 1957 as a start for working on my PhD thesis (Rosenfeld, 1961), I started paying home visits to people with psychiatric disorders who had applied for psychotherapy in a psychiatric outpatient clinic. I chose fifteen of these individuals proceeded to come to only one psychotherapy session (these I named "non-continuers"). The other fifteen, who had been "pair-matched", i.e. who had the same socio-economic qualities as the non-continuers did continue for at least ten sessions (hence their label of "continuers"). Without knowing so at the time, this project became my first study of the excluded in our midst, in this case, the ones who had not been able to accept the way in which the psychiatrist had offered them help. For the next four years, I engaged in what I later learned was "content analysis", of the more than six hundred documented "help-taking incidents" I had collected from the 30 PhD interviewees. The qualitative analysis I employed had not been systematically used by me and not by many others. My approach included identifying the unique kinds of help—including the types and styles of helpers, the problems and the kinds of help offered which made both groups of clients seek psychotherapy—from which the "continuers" had been able to benefit in the present since it was in line with ways in which they had been offered help in the past. This was not true for the "non-continuers" who had been offered the same kinds of help but these did not fit their expectations. During this research, understandings surfaced about the style of help and of helpers which may contribute to any particular client choosing to continue or discontinue psychotherapy. It highlighted the continuers' help-taking, which was in line with their expectations of what psychiatric services offered, but did not accord with the expectations of the non-continuers. To give one example: none of the fifteen non-continuers and nine of the continuers had, in their past, been helped by friends. This was an indication of how to help someone who turned to the kind of psychiatric help relevant for the continuers and not for the non-continuers. In contrast to the former, the latter expected their helpers to be persons who were older than them and not their contemporaries. Thus, this methodology gave information which enabled one to pave the way for offering psychiatric help which was attuned to the experiences and the expectations of the non-continuers.

This was one example of how I have used what I later got to know as "tacit knowledge" about un(der)served people as a key for learning about their needs along with and from them. This became what I later came to call "learning from success", which required ongoing learning so that what had worked in the past could be adopted and adapted for the future (Rosenfeld, 1992).

I have no doubt that this learning was a worthwhile undertaking. Yet I had to carry it out on my own and I needed to interest others in the insights I gained. Other people did not understand my research right away but put their trust both in me and this process of learning. This process took time and only culminated when, after four years of intensive work and two months before my scheduled return to Israel (where I was to take up a post at the newly established Paul Baerwald School of Social Work at the Hebrew University), I handed my thesis to the head of my PhD committee. Several weeks later, she summoned me to her office and asked me quite seriously, "Do you think that you really need a PhD?" in a tone devoid of venom, and in quite a matter-of-fact manner. Upon my asking what was wrong with it, she did not refer to the content at all and calmly stated that my style of writing and my English were unacceptable.

For some reason, perhaps because I had dared to do it in my own way, I took this news quite calmly. I sent a cable to the School of Social Work in Jerusalem, saying that I would only return for the second semester. I then proceeded to rope in my two previously-mentioned American friends, Ezra Levin and Elihu Katz, both of whom I had met on my first Saturday in

Chicago, to help me rewrite my thesis. Ezra, an observant Jew, not allowed to type on the "Succoth" Jewish holiday, agreed to dictate to me while I typed the corrections of my thesis.

Elihu, to whose family home I moved after my rental contract had ended, was erudite and, I admit, taught me then how to write an academic text. Six weeks later I resubmitted the thesis, and soon afterwards I was summoned to a meeting of my PhD committee. I remember that I entered the room quite calmly and was told with much reserve, "Your thesis is really quite good". That they spoke in such a manner came as no surprise to me as all four members of my committee were people with great integrity and were the kind who let me pass even if they remained somewhat puzzled by the topic of my thesis. I emphasize "puzzled" since the usual thinking at the time was how to change clients to suit services offered, while I had asked the opposite question: how could one adapt the services offered to the clients' needs?

They could not have known that my passion for my findings was connected to my pending return to Israel. Having started work with and about excluded people living with mental illness in the United States, I felt well-prepared and was looking forward to returning to Israel to apply what I had learned. I was quite content to do so after a six-year absence and with a clear agenda of my own. Although I did not know exactly what my next professional steps would be, I knew for sure that they would involve connecting with—and working for—the excluded in our society. In terms I would not have been able to use then, I had become resolved to focus my work on people who, because of the inaccessibility of opportunities to which they could have responded, were inevitably excluded. Indeed, the topic of my thesis (Rosenfeld, 1962) was a precursor of what will follow in the next sections of this book.

In addition, I think it should be made clear that at the time I could not explicitly formulate all my insights in terms of the conceptions I later put into words, such as "unleashing hidden potential", the "excluded", the "un(der)served in our midst", or by arguing that social workers and others tend to "invent interventions" based on the idea of "reciprocity" that would lead their clients beyond exclusion. As the title of my PhD thesis suggests, the population at risk who did not come to psychiatric outpatient treatment illustrates what one can learn about how not to bring about non-continuance of service.

## 4. WHEN AN OUTSIDER WHO BELONGS INITIATES MOVES BEYOND EXCLUSION

I came back to Israel in December 1961, after six special years in Chicago, to work at the newly founded and pioneering Paul Baerwald School of Social

Work at the Hebrew University of Jerusalem. This turned out to be an ideal opportunity for me, a budding social worker with few onerous obligations, to be offered a job where people had high expectations of me. In view of this, I knew it was up to me to find my way in what was a new place which I knew needed me and which also welcomed me.

At the school, beyond fulfilling my basic teaching duties, I was able to choose how to "invest in the production of service provisions" for the benefit of the "under-served". At the time it was far from taken for granted to conceptualize in terms that have by now become common in the academic and professional worlds. Today, I would say that what I was after was to provide opportunities for engaging researchers to use a language giving voice to both policy and practice so that each "world" could comprehend what the other was doing. And, at the same time, to seek out researchers with a methodology and with concepts suited to such mutual comprehension. This requires scholars prepared to engage in common language-bridging research and practice (Gal, 2013) (Strier, 2013).

While I know that at that time I also took on many other tasks, I became sure that by employing capacities for learning via what Schön calls "reflection in/on action", it would be possible to follow more and more what I would now call action-oriented "theories-in-use". Today I would refer to this idea as actions which are of benefit to the different "un(der)served in our midst". I had also called it providing "the excluded in our midst" with what would enable them to move towards reciprocity, towards being both benefactors and beneficiaries, those who received what they needed and of which they could use it. If that were not enough, through what they had benefited or through their personal affinities, all this had been of benefit also to the social worker.

That I could learn to work in this way was in no small part thanks to the "safe haven" I had found at this first-ever School of Social Work at an Israeli university where I had studied and in the country in which I felt so clearly at home. Moreover, I now believe that my sense of belonging and inclusion there were what enabled me to invest in whatever "the moves beyond exclusion" would be. Putting it in these terms enabled me to make this one of my major commitments upon my return to Israel. At that point, without any clear expectations that this would develop into a serious study about poverty or indeed about exclusion, I joined forces with my late colleague Lotte Salzberger and with Yehuda Matras, sociologist and demographer, in order to learn more about the lives of Jewish families living in Jerusalem, focusing on those called the "socially deprived", i.e. those living in poverty (Rosenfeld, Salzberger and Matras, 1973).

To provide an overall picture of the study, we interviewed approximately one thousand Jewish mothers in Jerusalem, as an easily accessible population in hospitals right after they had given birth. As it turned out, this would be the first study of families living in poverty in Israel (funded by the United States government). What, in hindsight, strikes me today, is the conspicuous omission of Arab mothers from the study.

There are four aspects of this study which were especially important:

1. Having "invented" the concept of "exigencies" as objective indicators of poverty.
2. Having studied the "predicaments" i.e. the subjective indicators of needs which each of the 1000 interviewees would identify.
3. Having made the unbelievable discovery that there were around three hundred (!) agencies which, at the time, contributed to the well-being of the then over 150,000 Jewish families in Jerusalem.
4. Having looked at these families in terms of their places of birth, countries of origins and year of immigration.

All these enabled us and any others to stop seeing the poor as anonymous beings rather than as partners.

At the "beginnings" of Israel as a new state and a society engaged in survival and in "absorbing" new immigrants, it took many years to acknowledge and to study poverty in Jerusalem among Jews and Arabs, and, among them, the ultra-religious Jews.

I believe that since I was both a social worker who had studied sociology and a psycho-therapist, I had the good sense to combine the public health-inspired study on the phenomenon of poverty in one society with that of a sub-group of twenty seven Jewish families living in poverty in Jerusalem (Rosenfeld, Morris and Salzberger, 1969).

The heart of the wider study was to connect the objective indicators of need—"exigencies"—with the subjective ones—"predicaments"—in order to explore who were the least well off and who, as it turned out, were those who tended not to declare subjective needs, i.e. did not expect help. One of the most interesting findings of this study showed that those who were most objectively in need, were also those who were least likely to expect help and thus to receive it. In contrast, the more well-off in that society were those who had relatively, and even objectively, a greater chance of receiving what they needed. And if that were not enough, it also became clear that those entrusted with providing help to those who needed it most were served by the least well qualified providers of services.

We presented this study at a conference sponsored by the United Nations European Office in 1972, where one of the main contributions to the conference was Père Borelli's enthusiastic and deeply caring talk about the street children on the slopes of Naples. In addition, thanks to Eyvind Hytten, the impressive Norwegian Head of the European Social Development Program Unit of the United Nations Office at Geneva, Père Joseph, the founder of the

Fourth World Movement, and I, were able to establish a partnership, if not friendship, that flourished after that conference. I subsequently attended many workshops and conferences on poverty and social exclusion and could thus make this topic one which helped develop a wider interest in poverty in Israel. Over time, thanks to these conferences, I began adopting the approach of listening carefully to studies of and with, rather than about, people living in poverty. These encounters also connected me deeply with the ATD Fourth World Movement[5], and hence, both to the poor themselves and to other members of ATD who had made serving "people living in poverty" and not "the poor" or "poverty", a lifetime pursuit to which I will refer later on.

For me, the importance of the study carried out in Israel was threefold:

First, it highlighted objectively, i.e. based on facts, that there was a striking disequilibrium between the quality and the accessibility of the kind and amount of help and provisions required by those living in poverty and the means and chances of their receiving them. This situation developed because the "unseen poor" who needed them most, were not in one's mind and thus beyond the reach of those who disposed of what these "others" needed or, rather, beyond what they were expected to want.

Second, it introduced the idea of two types of people living in poverty. On the one hand there are those who are poor and who are "unseen" and who make no claims and are, as such, less likely to move out of poverty. On the other hand, there are those who are perhaps equally poor but who assume that they have a claim, and therefore tend to claim what they needed and therefore have a greater chance to be served.

The third important contribution was that it put on the map those multiple services in the areas of health, education, income and labor which, in unison, were responsible for addressing the well-being of those living in poverty.

These insights do not mean that these are three modes of viewing society's responsibility for or obligations to address the needs of those living in poverty. However, they did create a language relevant for any society wanting to address the often unheard voices of those living in poverty and not just those who traditionally tend to be addressed in terms of employment, health, education and immigration, but not directly because of their poverty. In retrospect I understand that I had never before considered the existence and the prevalence of poverty or, for that matter, the possibility of people living in poverty in the 20-year-old State of Israel. This was because at that time the prevailing aura of socialism minimized the existence of poverty, and the idea of the Welfare State had only just been introduced into our society. At that time social work practice had all too rarely seen poverty per se, and especially those living in extreme poverty, as one of its areas of concern. Rather, social work at the time either simply did not see those living in poverty or at best saw them as to be little more than people "pitied" for their circumstances. With this in mind, psychoanalysis and psychotherapy were seen as unsuited for these individuals, and similarly at that time most social workers considered that such therapies could only be of service to the middle or upper-middle class.

There and then I had noted that being an outsider offers opportunities to study issues which insiders may not have, and on this issue I have written recently (Rosenfeld, 2015).

## 5. SERVING THE INDIVIDUAL AND THE COLLECTIVE: AN IRRESOLVABLE DILEMMA THAT LEADS TO LEARNING

Throughout my working life I found myself again and again confronting the dilemma of whom I should serve—the individual or the collective—or perhaps both of them? These remain dilemmas with which I have learned to live, without resolution. That they became so relevant has to do with the nature of the society in which I worked. Israel as a state and as a society is constantly torn between addressing the needs of the individual and demanding responsibility for the collective from the individual. This dynamic has been of special importance in the life of the kibbutz, where so much revolved around the fact that the kibbutz is a collective. Consequently, as a collective it has responsibility for serving both the interests of the collective and of its individual members. In another context, I was confronted with this issue in the Israeli Army where service is compulsory and where the contribution of the collective to the individual and the individual to the collective is problematic. For me, as a mental health officer, I inevitably considered the contribution of the collective to the individual to be more relevant.

I personally had encountered these dilemmas since we had arrived in Palestine, where each of us was expected to contribute to the new society at a time when the matter of what society owed to the individual remained less clear. But then I tried to address what I expected of myself together with what others expected of me. While serving in the military in the newly-established Israeli Defense Force I had pursued paths that taught me to care for others without neglecting myself. In the army in particular, I saw how being of service could benefit both the army as a collective and any individual, often regardless of his/her strengths or shortcomings. These kinds of reciprocal opportunities were the concern of soldiers who both contributed to and benefited from the collective. I wrote an article about this entitled "Serving the Individual and the Collectives: Lessons from the Wars of Israel" (Rosenfeld 1980). At the risk of self-promotion, I think that this essay was seminal in the sense of charting out how military service provided opportunities for each to pave his/her way. At the time, this was a rather original idea, given that it stood in stark contrast to the prevailing national ideology of serving the collective.

This issue has also concerned me with regard to communism and socialism in terms of their concern for the individual, where the collective is so dominant. In the course of my grappling with this issue, I found two relevant responses or solutions. The first was from the Yugoslav Professor Eugen Pusić, who somewhat cynically had stated that "the difference between socialism and capitalism is that under capitalism, man is exploited by man, and under socialism it is the other way around." The second refers to what I heard from a Chinese student whom I met in Hong Kong in the mid-seventies. His observation was that, "under communism the individual serves the collective and under capitalism the collective serves the individual." Both of these reflections remained equally relevant to my ongoing concern about this ever-present and irresolvable dilemma in democratic societies. This I had learned how uninformed and equivocal so many, including myself, were about what extreme poverty was all about.

I put all these qualms aside after I had met Père Joseph Wresinski, the founder of the ATD Fourth World Movement, in 1970 at a Conference in Bienne, Switzerland. His action-oriented challenge was for collectives to join forces for the benefit of the previously unseen and unheard—individuals and groups that had been betrayed by the societies they lived in. I came to see this as an opportunity for all and not just for some of us, and it resolved my dilemma with regard to serving both the individual and the collective. I tried to be both a beneficiary and a benefactor. To do so became possible when I dared to introduce the ideas of reciprocity, if not tenderness and intimacy, into the lives of any of the "stakeholders"—nay partners—involved, be it as individuals or collectives, be it as clients or members of service organizations. Doing so often enabled both partners, often after a period of time, to move on and not remain imprisoned by reciprocal estrangement. This outcome can occur when the excluded, on the one hand, and those who have excluded them, on the other, are helped to deal with this gap and to experience their own authentic, though often hidden, pain and helplessness which tend to stand in the way of new beginnings. It is this major dilemma which leads to ongoing learning.

## 6. ON PSYCHOANALYSIS AND SOCIAL WORK AS THE KEY FOR INITIATING PERSONAL AND PROFESSIONAL RECIPROCITY IN THE PRESENT AND THUS FOR THE FUTURE

> Yesterday is history.
> Tomorrow is a mystery.
> And today? Today is a gift.
> That's why we call it the present
> —Attributed to Eleanor Roosevelt

As mentioned before, there were two spheres of commitment stemming from my parents' influence and it was that dilemma that had shaped my life from early on. The first was my father's deep commitment to Zionism determined its investment in the establishment of a Jewish State as "the" way for being authentically Jewish. The other, a somewhat later influence, was that of psychoanalysis, which was a personal interest of my mother and her circle of friends. Both of these spheres of action, as well as playing music and shelves full of books in my parental home, that were part of our lives that had had an impact on my becoming a social worker and a psychoanalytically oriented psychotherapist for whom reciprocity is at the heart of human transactions (Douglas, 2007).

Looking back, I see that over time this is what I had become increasingly able to be and that this is at the roots of my commitment to both social work and psychoanalysis. What both have in common is that the calling of both these personal human services lies in seeing the quest for reciprocity as an ongoing search for who you are, for furthering what is unique and authentic to each individual and beyond it, even to any group, collective or organization. Since a primary mission of social work is to serve the un(der)served in our midst, i.e. to enable those who live in exclusion to move beyond it, and it is that that had determined considering the need of each of them and not to them as a collective. It is this recognition which brought about first the initiation and then the introduction to what we refer here in terms of reciprocity. By reciprocity we refer to having or gaining partners from whom, at one and the same time, we can both benefit and also to be of benefit (Rosenfeld, 1980). Hence, since the domain of social work is the lives of those living in exclusion, its mission is to pave their ways beyond exclusion by enabling all involved to experience reciprocity.

In contrast, the contribution of psychoanalysis to reciprocity derives, I believe, from its specific mission of getting acquainted with and being served by one's unconscious. This process, among others, also paves the way for becoming who one can become and be. In other terms, both social work and psychoanalysis engage in unleashing what we have called people's hidden potential (Defraigne-Tardieu, 2002). On this basis, what both psychoanalysis-psychotherapy on the one hand, and social work on the other, have in common: Each in its own way, provides opportunities for any collective or individual to find their voice, to be seen, and to become more and more able to shape their lives. Because of this, each of them is, with or without acknowledgement, consciously or unconsciously, able to become beneficiaries of those they serve.

Indeed, both psychoanalysis and psychotherapy on the one hand, and social work on the other, are professions whose transactions contain elements of reciprocity. Without expanding on it here, it is a rarely mentioned similarity between them which I base on my own personal and professional experience.

The following are four opportunities from which I have learned:

The first is related to my experience as a patient who throughout his life has spent many hours with quite a few psychoanalysts and psychoanalytically oriented professionals. Over time, I have been enabled to move beyond some of the hardships to which I had been exposed. To do so, I have been enabled by working through what had been in the past and to advance beyond so as to live in the present.

Second, throughout my experience as a patient I benefited from the commitment of most of my therapists which surely contributed to my capacities to be and remain an effective learner. These capacities gave me the opportunity to engage in ongoing learning as a "social activist" and who, as such, had also been able to benefit from the inherent differences between my various professional pursuits. Because of that, I knowingly did not join those who use the study of social work primarily as a springboard for becoming psychotherapists.

Third, is my unceasing gratitude for having been exposed to and to learn from the powers of the unconscious and what is vested in it. Once I had discovered this process, it enabled me to benefit from what initially may have seemed hidden in many of my pursuits. Accordingly, I have invested in an incessant search for transforming what is hidden—i.e. "tacit"—into actionable and explicit knowledge so as not to resort to blaming others for not being able to serve them or, alternatively, concentrating on failures. Indeed, this acquaintance with the unconscious, has clearly also led me to somewhat knowingly focus on "learning from success" where I had found out that like benefitting from the unconscious, learning how to unearth tacit knowledge which had been "hidden" *is* of enormous benefit. At times learning from success is also related to social workers' becoming aware and acknowledging its roots in their own personal unconscious. In a closely related way, it may well be that it is this acknowledgement that enables one to dare experience one's own and other people's helplessness which is often so essential for enabling one to know, for instance, that sometimes there is no chance to offer help, or do more than acknowledge the helplessness connected to it.

Fourth, and last but not least, the connection between social work and psychoanalysis is at the root of my readiness to dare discover and "look evil in the eye" as a point of departure for exploring evil both when related to one's own well-being, but also for the benefit of that of the "others". While Adam Smith said that "pity and compassion are words appropriated to signify our fellow-feeling with the sorrow of others", (Smith, 1759), I believe that it takes one's own generosity in terms of one's own fellow-feeling for the wellbeing of both oneself and any other to unearth such evil (Brazelton, Kostowsky and Main, 1974). To do so, does indeed require being ready to accept one's own or any others' evil, also because it enables one to attend the well-being, the success of one's own and of any other's capacities for leading a good life.

Indeed, I had become able to prepare myself for doing so via investing in "learning from success", which is quite a journey. Suffice it to say that whatever may be the rationale for considering the acceptance of what we have done as being evil, it provides a basis for generosity, sorrow and pleasure rather than for pity and compassion and this is based on discovering the barriers of the past to pave the way for a different future. This after all is what "learning from success" is all about. In fact, there is evidence from psychoanalysis and psychotherapy to knowingly consider and acknowledge these turning-points which lead to a different future rather than being hang-ups dominated by the past. It is this understanding that has led to my interest, though for a long time unknowingly, in "ongoing learning" as an opportunity for the "good life". This was not only due to my continuing curiosity from early on in psychoanalysis and psychotherapy but also from my early opportunity of reading the books about these topics that were in my parents' rich library. I remember reading *Wayward Youth* by August Aichhorn (1935), which was all about "caring treatment" and *"I Never Promised you a Rose Garden"*, on which I had written in section I.3 which had made an indelible impression on me. The latter was written by Joan Greenberg (1964), the pseudonym of a very rich patient whose analyst was the well-known psychoanalyst Frieda Fromm Reichmann. What made such an ineradicable impression on me was how the analyst responded when the by-then-well-served patient who was reluctant to rejoin what seemed to her to be a cruel world was told by her analyst: "I never promised you a rose garden. I only promised you to understand". It was that which had reconnected me with Freud's well-known statement that "the voice of the intellect is a soft one, but it does not rest until it has gained a hearing". This implies that it takes a while to make sense of what one had understood to have a beneficial impact, something that is not only relevant to therapy but to life as well. Moreover, that this psychoanalyst could have said this to her formerly seriously sick patient, had affirmed for me, then for the first time, that psychoanalysis need not be a cool, distant and impersonal undertaking and that what can be learned from it and psychotherapy, can and may also be in line with the commitment of social work to help the least well-served-in-our-midst both with persistence and with dedication, and without a quest for glamour, and also with readiness to keep being engaged in "ongoing learning" rather than being paralyzed by an ongoing commitment to ideas and theories of the past in an ever changing world.

The close link between psychoanalysis and psychotherapy on the one hand and social work on the other lies in both being and becoming authentic human services, each with its own "calling". For the former two, it is primarily to the wellbeing of individuals and groups and for the latter—social work—it is also for deploying "reciprocity". It is because of these differences that training for each has to be dissimilar; each one requiring its own mode of learning and development. It is this understanding that had led me to neither see social work training as a point of departure for engaging in psychotherapy nor the other way around. This, since in social work the primary emphasis is on reciprocity, rather than on attachment, which is a primary basis and conviction which has often been named "dyadic therapy". This enabled me to realize that reciprocity might also be relevant for psychotherapy and psychoanalysis, and then, when this is the case, also the most excluded in our midst, those served by social work, could benefit from psychotherapy and psychoanalysis. That reciprocity *is* a possible component of psychotherapeutic treatment is in line with John Dewey's notion related to considering both transactions *and* interactions being part of psychotherapeutic treatment, i.e. also transactions which have an impact on each. Introducing reciprocity into psychoanalysis may enable its practitioners to openly acknowledge its benefits also for themselves. Put more succinctly: an initial readiness for reciprocity may enable psychotherapists and psychoanalysts, for instance, to let go of adherence to what is at times excessively hierarchical and doctrinaire, mainly "transference", and may enable patient and therapist to own up to what had been achieved by each in the course of their joint work, without considering it being counter transferential, i.e. caught in the past.

One clear illustration of what in this context is at the heart of reciprocity can be found in "Fugitive Pieces" (Michaels, 1997). There the person who had come to save a child during the Holocaust turned out to be the one who was saved by the child thereby being an example of how reciprocity works for the benefit of both parties. Thus the impact of psychotherapy and psychoanalysis would not only be in serving the other, but in practitioners benefitting not just financially but also in terms of knowledge that their patients have contributed to them and to their work as a therapist. Once recognizing that their "patients" may have something to contribute to psychotherapy and psychoanalysis, social workers may be ready to struggle for the latter's relevance and not just as their well-wishers and benefactors but also as the excluded in our midst which they were or are. This is reflected in some of the more recent writings on these topics (Astor 2000) (Gammelgaard 2010).

## NOTES

*Defraigne-Tardieu (2002).
  1. Rosenfeld, 1964.
  2. I had thought that the pianist Richard Goode had said this, but as he wrote to me he "couldn't remember having said this and thinks [he] might use it in the future".
  3. The first time that I came across the idea around the research carried out by Ripple and her colleague (1953) who carried out research on motivation, capacity and opportunity –

opportunity client and helper, and from it I deduced that "opportunity service" should be considered as the independent variable to be studied (Rosenfeld, 1962).
 4. See Part V.
 5. Appendix I.

# IV

# On Trails towards "Learning from Success": Seven Examples

INTRODUCTION: SEVEN PURSUITS WHICH IN RETROSPECT WAS AN UNEXPECTED PRECURSOR OF "LEARNING FROM SUCCESS"

> There are multiple sources of knowledge
> for "explaining the world"
> or for that of "changing it" (Argyris)[1]

In the context of my life's work, my focus has been on changing the world rather than on explaining it. However, the sources for change-oriented knowledge in so many situations are often quite limited. Hence, "learning from success" has not only been effective but is also an opportunity not to be wasted. The successful methodologies of learning from success were developed over the last two decades by the Unit for the Learning from Success and Ongoing Learning in the Human Services (see Appendix II), which is part of the Myers-JDC-Brookdale Institute in Jerusalem. There, our focus has been on identifying what Argyris and Schön have called "tacit knowledge", knowledge describing effective actions and, on that basis, the "principles of actions" that brought about change in the past and which in similar contexts, may become guidelines for what to do in the present and thus for the future (Chaskin and Rosenfeld, 2008).

What is worth mentioning are the unforeseen commonalities derived from the seven accounts of what I refer to as "the move from exclusion to reciprocity". In each there is an implied reference to the initiation of what is called "reciprocity" which is then followed by its introduction, of that that has brought about change in the lives of the excluded. In those terms, reciprocity is both what initiates change and what brings it about. Hence the focus of this section on "learning from success" is on identifying actions which have initiated the move beyond exclusion and those actions which have enabled the process of change, i.e. of success in terms of actions that have brought about the move from exclusion to reciprocity. Both these activities started out as "tacit knowledge" from the past and were explicated, i.e. became actionable knowledge in the present and for the future. The awareness of both of these components of both "learning from success" and the move from exclusion to reciprocity dawned on me as an afterthought.

## 1. TRAINING OF AIR FORCE PILOTS IN ISRAEL (1954-55): HOW TO PUT AN END TO EXCESSIVE FLUNKING OF CADETS

One of my early studies and the first sociological one in the Israeli Air Force concerned the training of cadets around 1954-55, several years after the establishment of the State. At that time, the power of the collective within the army was still very great and hence the establishment of hierarchical structures was problematic. When the number of cadets graduating to be pilots became exceedingly low, it raised the alarm of General Dan Tolkovsky, then head of the Israeli Air Force. He broached the subject with his friend, Professor Shmuel Eisenstadt, the head of the Department of Sociology at the Hebrew University of Jerusalem, who was my teacher and personal friend.

Shmuel turned to three of his students, the late Eliezer Rosenstein, Moshe Lissak and myself, suggesting that we meet the staff responsible for the training of pilots. We met these highly impatient trainers who openly complained that they hated their jobs and wanted to return to being "real" pilots. They felt isolated and abandoned by their commanders and were openly envious and hostile towards the cadets, whom they considered to be the ones who prevented them from flying.

We were amazed by the way Eisenstadt addressed the matter. Based on his experience and intuition, he understood that the excessive flunking of cadets had to do with the envy of the trainers. Then, at the meeting with us and the trainers, when this shrewd Head of the Air Force entered the room, he told the trainers and their commanders the following story which, as we shall see, illustrated his understanding of the situation: "There once was a young man who had a girlfriend. They lived together, but he did not want to marry. Then, one day, he had to marry her because she had become pregnant". And he added: "You see, he had no choice but to marry. You the trainers are the only ones in charge of training the cadets. So, the Israeli Army has no choice, neither do you." He stalked out of the room after telling the Head of the Training School to see to it that each of the trainers be given more opportunities to fly his own plane. He said so because he too considered the lack of such opportunities to be one possible explanation for their tendency to fail so many cadets. Soon afterwards the number of cadets in training who became pilots rose significantly.

In addition there was one more event which I can never forget. After the meeting, the head trainer and two others were told to invite each of us for a flight in a military plane. The head of the trainers came up to me, the senior of us three, and asked me to follow him to his plane. He was far from a totally sweet man and, when we were in the air, he turned the plane, and thus us, upside down. While this was happening, he told me over the earphone in an exceedingly calm voice: "so you can see now what a "spin" is all about," and soon after, he made the plane dance. Being totally overwhelmed and frightened, while playing it cool, I asked him in a trembling voice over the earphone: "Is that the Sharon Hotel down there?" He mumbled: "Yes", turned the plane around and landed it right away. Down on the ground, with me scarcely knowing where I was, he told his colleagues with total cool: "When I showed him what a "spin" was, that bastard asked me whether the spin had been over the Sharon Hotel." After that, he went off without saying good bye. This however was not so terrible since I could use the time to weigh whether and in what way we had made a positive contribution to the Israeli Air Force which, as it turned out, we had.

In retrospect, I recognize what had happened. The Head of the Air Force understood that the trainers needed to see that he was concerned about them, which would enable them to do their job so that the air force could have its pilots. At the time I would not have named this "learning from success". But that is what it was. It happened after the Head of the Air Force had transformed "hidden knowledge"—the envy of the trainers—into actionable terms, which would give the envious trainers opportunities to fly their own planes and to become acquainted with their envy. By his highlighting both his insights—the trainers feeling neglected and their envy of the cadets—he contributed to furthering the desired result: not to flunk the cadets. This then was the success of our joint learning and a precursor of what was to come.

## 2. SERVING FAMILIES OF SAILORS IN THE ISRAELI MERCHANT MARINE, 1964[2]

A decade later, in the early sixties, my late friend Eliezer Rosenstein and his colleague Bilha Manheim[3] from the Department of General Studies at the

Technion of Haifa, approached me, as someone who had experience as a Mental Health Officer in the Israeli Army, to launch a study on a seemingly different problem. It was to be the first Israeli study of families of sailors. Sponsored by the Social Services of the Israeli Merchant Marine, it became known as the "Study of the Long Week-End", which referred to the few days of the weekend during which the usually-absent father—the sailor—came to join his family. Their request was to establish services for a population of sailor families whose circumstances were quite different from those families connected to the Army or the Police. After we discovered what was unique about the life of these families, our study came to provide a new focus for the future work of this social service.

In preparation for this study, Eliezer and I went separately on cruises to Europe on a merchant marine ship. Around the same time Bilha interviewed some of these families in their homes.

Initially we were convinced that all that was needed was something like the services provided for soldiers, policemen or commercial pilots, but we were taken by surprise to discover that these families had two unique hardships. The first was that when the mother remained alone with the children, she was the sole person in charge of them, the home, and all other matters related to the family. She generally had few social contacts, being a go-between and not a partner with anyone, and felt a deep sense of loneliness. The second involved the unpredictably shorter or longer presences of the father on shore, called "long week-ends". These times were marked by both a feeling of unsettledness and a longing for the relative tranquility to descend again on the home when the father went back to sea. If that were not enough, during the weeks of his absence the separation from him was experienced as a period of relief.

Additionally, during the "long week-ends" the sailor was torn between his "duties" on board the ship in port and his "obligation" to make contact with his immediate family and with those around it. It was usually a period of ongoing transitions related to mutual re-adjustments between family members and one in which there was a weigh-up between spoiling the children and exercising authority that was frequently lacking. Moreover, it was also a period when the longed-for and seemingly welcome father made demands that tended to be resented by those whom he had left behind and whom he was to leave again.

In light of this, it was difficult to know what services should be provided to the family and the sailor, both when he was at sea and at home. As it turned out, when they were ostensibly together at home and when the husband was at sea, both partners felt abandoned and alone.

Once we understood and conveyed this situation to the social welfare services for members of the Merchant Marine *and* their families, they were able to discard preconceived ideas about the conventional meaning of a father's absence. By this we enabled them to call their services "welfare services for sailors and their families". This freed them to discover the particular needs of the families and thus the specific ways for serving them appropriately during those all too long weekends with the husband and their guilt-ridden relief after his departure. In fact, it demanded a shift in their mindset towards considering the father's presence and the "long week-ends", no longer as a desired and desirable "time out", as one had thought and sought.

At the time, it seemed sufficient to point out that the preconceived nature of the life of these families had to be modified. Hence we suggested clarifying together with the families how they felt when the father was absent, when they were all together, and how one could openly explore the impact of this kind of life on the family members. Soon after having written our report, we parted company with the Social Welfare Services for the Merchant Marine Sailors and their Families with the sense that at least we did not have much to offer.

All I can say in retrospect is that had the study been done at a time when the "learning from success" methodology was available, we would have taken the time to learn how these services might be adapted to the specific needs of these sailors and their families.

## 3. THE UNPREDICTED MOBILITY OF BOYS FROM A LOW-INCOME COMMUNITY: WHICH PATTERNS OF PARENTING MADE THEIR RESILIENCY POSSIBLE?[4]

In 1976 I was asked for the first time to assess a PhD thesis to do with the resiliency of certain youths in a low income community in Israel, who, despite their similar social backgrounds, had achieved what most youths in the same neighborhood had not. I was more than grateful for having been asked to read this thesis, that dealt with this persistently disregarded and for me ground-breaking topic. Its author was a socially committed sociologist by the name of Amilia Aviel (later Dinai), with whom I have been in contact ever since.

Her thesis, entitled: "Boys in a Neighborhood, Everyday Life in Hatikva Neighborhood" (Aviel, 1976) focused on a lower class community in Tel Aviv.

Based on eighteen months of participant observations, Aviel classified the families there according to three modes of parenting in relating to their sons. These were "warm families", "concerned families" and "neglecting families". The boys who were the most successful in terms of social mobility were those who had grown up in "warm families". They were those who later studied in high school, or, at least, were able to maintain steady work. Most of these boys also belonged to youth movements and some had steady girlfriends from outside the neighborhood, and later on they also dared to leave the Hatikva neighborhood during their adolescence and found their way in the army as only few others from the neighborhood had done. Thus, in our terms, they could be considered of high social mobility and, knowing their familial background, they could offer a guideline on how to initiate other families moving beyond exclusion and, from this vantage point, to become "successful" (Rosenfeld, 1996).

In contrast to boys from "concerned" and "neglecting" families, those from "warm" ones, had parents who were active partners, i.e. involved in their schoolwork, their well-being, and in extending hospitality to friends. In these families interactions were full of personal concern, mutual respect and among siblings, there was readiness to help. The parents in these families encouraged their children to adopt modern values, despite the fact that they themselves came from traditional homes. Indeed, they expressly told them that those values were important for the success of their sons. Similarly, they also urged their children to join youth movements and other organizations outside their neighborhood. These youth adapted better to the army, often acquiring military professions and completing their whole period of service, and later left this neighborhood and parental homes (Mash, 1987).

These findings certainly constituted a basis for highlighting what "learning from success" in the sphere of the mobility of these boys requires. However, at the time my colleagues and I did not yet attempt to look for action-oriented "independent" variables that could enable those interested in introducing social mobility and social "adjustment" via parents, teachers and others beyond this study.

What strikes me so many years later was that the formal social ideology at the time was not to ensure mobility, but social integration. At that time, and since the beginning of the State, information that might induce social mobility, like the findings of these studies, was ignored and not put to use. The idea was not to foster social mobility but to ensure the "integration", also called the "absorption", of multiple cultures of the different immigrant groups to this country. The idea of fostering mobility emerged much later.

## 4. WHEN A CRISIS IS AN OPPORTUNITY: WHAT ENABLED NEW YORK FAMILIES WHOSE HOMES BURNED DOWN TO ACHIEVE A BETTER LIFE

In line with my interest in "positive deviance", to learn from those who had unexpectedly done well, I used part of my time as a Visiting Professor at the School of Social Work at Columbia University in New York in 1979-80 to carry out, together with Professor Alaine Krim of the School, a pilot study of fifteen families living in the slums of New York whose houses were burned down by landlords intent on receiving insurance money (Rosenfeld and Krim, 1983). As it turned out, some of these families, in contrast to expectations, led a better life after the fire had forced them to leave their houses than they led before. In fact, nine of these fifteen mainly mono-parental families were generally better off than before. The objective indicators of this were whether the mothers had started work and/or study for the first time in their lives; the subjective indicators were what they stated, that is, that they were better off after the fire than before (Rosenfeld and Krim, 1983).

In the aftermath of the fire, the successes of these nine families, in contrast to the other six, related to the following three areas:

1. They had left the slum quarters where their families of origin remained.
2. The mothers tended to allow their children to act as the mothers' caretakers.
3. They believed that they were somehow special. As one mother had stated "I always knew that somebody up there liked me." These were the words she used to highlight the fact that she had been treated well in her youth.

None of these three findings applied to the six mothers who were no better, or even worse off, after the fire and this made us conclude the following:

On the basis of the first finding we tried to encourage and enable social workers to realize that improving the lives of slum dwellers would require opposing the prevalent policies tending to enable families to stay in their communities. This meant encouraging future families to leave the slums after the fire, something that stood in contrast to the assumed importance of following the so called "familial roots" policy, i.e. aiding them to stay in their excluded neighborhoods.

The second finding, relates to fostering mutually caring relationships between parents and children, which stands in contrast to insisting that parents be the sole caretakers. The fact that children can contribute to their mothers is rarely if ever taken into account by social workers. In this vein, not by chance, a university course about "the contribution of children to their parents" has been recently introduced at Tel Aviv University.

In line with the third finding, the sense of having had or not having had somebody who cared for the mothers in their youth was rarely something to which social workers paid attention in serving these mothers.

However different these three findings were, they tended not to be in tune, if not necessarily opposed to, the nature of what social workers tended to do in their work with these families (and not only in New York). Even though these findings are based on a pilot study, I believe that they might still be considered of relevance in any work with families living in other slum neighborhoods, and not only those whose homes had burned down. This because there is so little information available about any of them, and furthermore, as this study shows that one can learn from the success of even a few families. Even though I do not know what could have been done with these findings in the aftermath of this study, this information encouraged me to focus my and my colleagues' attention on what "learning from success" implies: to learn from what had worked in the past as an indicator, if not a directive, for what could be learned from similar action-oriented studies. This seems to be preferable to primarily focusing on studies that explain, rather than on those focusing primarily on presenting concrete forms of actions and policies which is what the "learning from success" method does.

It is for this reason that I believe that the "learning from success" ideas and methodologies would contribute to the well-being of any "un(der)served in our midst" and not just to them. This also convinced us to stress the importance of ongoing-learning. The latter has to be at the disposal of those who are entrusted with serving these often extraordinarily and needy families that come to the attention of social workers and who only because of the social worker's commitment to deliberately engage in learning is not likely to be well received.

I end here by describing what happened to me towards the end of this study when I was still in New York and about to return to Israel. The last of the fifteen mothers I was to interview, "Mrs. Roberts", was one of those who had benefited from the fire and done better after her house burned down. With that expectation I called out for "Mrs. Roberts" to enter my room. In came a woman with a girl whom I expected to be caring for her mother. However what happened was that Mrs. Roberts commanded her daughter saying such things as "Say hello to the Uncle, bow to him". It soon turned out that this was the wrong "Mrs. Roberts", someone not belonging to the study group. To my great relief, the other "Mrs. Roberts" came, somewhat late, and asked to be seen by me. When she came in, quite upset, her daughter said solicitously, "Why are you crying again, mummy?" Saying this clearly meant that she was attentive to her mother, which did not only relieve my concern for the wrong "Mrs. Roberts", but made me think that we were on the right track.

What remains noteworthy, even in retrospect, is that even the most deprived families may benefit from moving their home rather than staying in the neighborhood in which their isolation and exclusion was generated. In those terms, something could be learned from the successes of those mothers who had benefited from the fire by moving out of their restricted living conditions in their original neighborhood.

The insights gained from the readiness for learning from success of families who need to be served after one particular crisis might well enable social workers to learn from the successes of those for whom their crises turned out to be an opportunity.

## 5. ON FORCED EVACUATIONS: FROM SINAI (1982) AND THEN THE GAZA STRIP (2005)

There are many kinds of forced evacuations of populations, including those resulting from crises related to climate, hydroelectric dams, or even "peace treaties". One thing that is common to all kinds of evacuations is that, in their aftermath, there are always some populations who tend to be ignored and who then become the "victims" of these events. Two such evacuations of Israeli settlers have occurred in the history of the State. First, when the government decided in 1982 to leave the Sinai Peninsula (Moses, Hrushovski, Rosenfeld and Beumel, 1982) (Rosenfeld, Moses, Hrushovski and Beumel, 1985) (Moses, Rosenfeld, Hrushovski-Moses, 1987) and then again, in 2005, to withdraw from the Gaza Strip (Rosenfeld, Rosenberg and Elek, 2010). These evacuations were deeply resented by most of the evacuees and by many other people in Israel. In view of this, colleagues and I decided to try to contribute to learning on how to ease the way for the evacuees. This was for both psycho-social reasons on the one hand, and political reasons on the other. The latter was because we considered these withdrawals as a step towards advancing peace between Israel and the Palestinians. Whatever the motivations for initiating this work, in order to contribute to the well-being of evacuees, it was also geared towards increasing the likelihood of future evacuations, efforts which, not surprisingly, were disapproved of by various political entities.

### On the evacuation from the Sinai Peninsula (1982)

In 1981/2, my late friends Rafael and Rena Moses, he a psychiatrist and both of them psychoanalysts, along with Reuven Beumel and I, both social workers, offered to head a study about what the Sinai evacuation might mean for its evacuees and how one might ease their plight. For this purpose, the government authorities responsible for the evacuation flew us to Ophira, now Sharm-el-Sheikh, in the Sinai Peninsula, which was subsequently returned to Egypt.

During our repeated visits there, we soon found out that for most of the population scheduled to be evacuated this move was like being expelled from "The Garden of Eden" because life there had been so unusually pastoral and peaceful. Upon meeting different groups of evacuees, we found that many considered the evacuation as an expulsion. There were actually four different sub-groups of evacuees who became the focus of our research. However, even though it quickly became apparent that beyond learning about the impact of the evacuation on the evacuees through speaking with teachers and leaders at the time of evacuation, there was very little we could do for their benefit in the midst of the evacuation itself. But we did hope to learn from it for the benefit of those to be evacuated in the future.

The first group we identified consisted of people who had moved to the Sinai largely for financial reasons, i.e. who had had no resources previously and who were relocated from the Sinai after they had improved their *socioeconomic situation* during their lives there. Thus, when they received significant financial compensation to pave their way back, many reported feeling overwhelmed. There were even some who went out and bought goods just before the evacuation in order to show people from the neighborhoods they had originally left how well off they had become.

While recognizing their need to emphasize how they had blossomed in Sinai, we tried to help the service organizations in aiding the evacuees to come to terms with the pending change, i.e. to help them leave the past behind and prepare for their future, for their post-evacuation lives. This approach recognized that they invested in showing off to their former-neighbors how well they had made it, rather than investing time in thinking how to make their way back to Israel where they had come from and to where they were about to return.

There was a second and quite different group, who were practical about the evacuation. They prepared themselves for their "return to Israel with grief". But they, in contrast to many others, did it with a minimum of resentment. They tried to make the most of the compensation money, looking for the best alternatives for making their way back in the State of Israel.

The third group were people who had gone to the Sinai after they had lived through the Holocaust. This group reported feeling totally helpless. They felt that now they were being evicted for a second time—and this—by their own people. This group was seriously confused and felt betrayed but now not by their enemies. It was the one group which we felt we could not help, beyond alerting them and others to what would be difficult on their way out.

A fourth group consisted of those who knowingly or openly opposed the evacuation only in its aftermath, in the wake of the hardships they suffered following it. At that point, once they had settled back in Israel, they felt a sense of betrayal and abandonment. They found that they had to build their own new lives with little support from either their new local authorities or the national bodies in charge of the evacuation. We experienced this personally when, following the evacuation, one of our hosts who was a local leader, abruptly cut off contact with us. In hindsight, it appeared that he had done so because he felt betrayed by us hoping that, after the good contact we had been able to establish with him, we might continue to be with him after the evacuation, upon returning to Israel. We had not talked about this, and, indeed, we had never thought that these people would feel abandoned by us also. In the aftermath it became apparent that they had begun to identify us as affiliated with the government who, in their eyes, were responsible for some of their and others' hardship on and after their return. The shift took place when leaders like the one I have mentioned began having their own resettlement difficulties and subsequently found themselves identifying with the other "returnees", none of whom felt too welcome back in Israel. If that were not enough, these were the local leaders who had served as representatives of the Israeli government in matters to do with the logistics of the evacuation, and who afterwards had suddenly found themselves feeling like traitors who had sold out their neighbors and who themselves had found it hard to readjust. Like many other evacuees they came to feel that they had colluded with the authorities during the evacuation and they too began to feel helpless and perplexed and whose ideals had been betrayed.

After the evacuation, all researchers, including us, presented our findings on the four groups of evacuees in order to be of use in any later evacuations. A common, major finding in the aftermath of the evacuation of the Sinai was that some of the researchers felt like collaborators who had agreed to be paid by the victors for their research. This despite the fact that they may have contributed to making any future evacuation happen more smoothly.

The following findings were presented after the evacuation by several researchers. At that time both the presenters and those who had been informants, each for their own reasons, were reluctant to publicize their findings and thus we decided to summarize four of the common themes agreed upon. The themes were:

a. The reliving of previous deportations.
b. The fear of returning to where they had come from.
c. A variety of symptoms when they came to facing this, as a second evacuation.
d. A marked, sometimes massive denial of the pending evacuation[5].

The following statement was presented on the morning of March 21, 1982, by Israel's civil administration on the Southern part of the Sinai Peninsula, just before the evacuation.

> The dreaded moment is here. Here we stand looking around us, at our homes, at this patch of land we have learned to love so much. We cannot believe that all of this has happened. It seems unimaginable that the next time we drive away it will be with our one-way ticket, never again to return to our homes, to our beloved Ophira...[6]
>
> We are the ones who were considered "crazy" when we first agreed to come to this forsaken spot. We made a new beginning in this unknown place, welding what we value in modern civilization with the majesty of the desert

and the seas. We were working not for ourselves only, but also for our fellow human beings in Israel, and beyond it. All this we are forced to give up, to evacuate our homes, to leave behind us all that we have built and wrought. Yet, that is not enough; not only do we have to leave, we must hand this place over to those who will come, as if we had so willed it . . . as though we had not tilled it and invested it with our souls . . . in another few days we may—at best—be given the chance to come back sometime as strangers visiting our own homes.

We decry a peace which uproots us from our homes. Yet with all our pain we know that we are necessary victims of Israel's search for an end to belligerency, for normal relations with our neighbors . . . .

. . . we leave here, proud that we were able to live our life as a community up to the last moment, that to the very end we were able to maintain our cultural, social and educational activities in a manner which many might have wished to emulate.

So we say shalom—our peace-as-goodbye. We all wish and desire that our personal sacrifice, the high price which our country is paying will not be in vain.

Farewell then, and may all of us fare well, wherever we go.

## On the Evacuation from the Gaza Strip (2005)

In contrast to the former study, one of the particular reasons for our conducting this research project was to increase the chance for peace by using what we had learned, in order to smooth the way for the evacuees in future evacuations. We and other researchers considered it a great achievement that, in light of what we had learned earlier, this next evacuation was much calmer. Indeed, the 2005 evacuation from the Gaza Strip was different and so much smoother than that from the Sinai. This was because it could be much more thoughtfully prepared, because it could also take into account the findings of our own and others' research during the Sinai evacuation. While as researchers, it reinforced our sense that learning from one evacuation can greatly benefit future evacuations and its evacuees, even though this may also have to do with the different political circumstances and the quite different characteristics of the evacuees in both evacuations. This was true even though in both cases most of the evacuees were ardently religious families who opposed policies that supported their return from the so-called "occupied territories". While in both evacuations the government tried to hand back the territories without violence or bloodshed, this one could be better managed.

Indeed, in preparing the Gaza evacuation, a great deal was invested in training the army and the police on how to avoid unnecessary confrontations. This was done, for instance, by distributing compensations in the course of the evacuation and recruiting educational experts who were deployed in order to prepare the children for what was to come. The central government had also left it in the hands of the local authorities to accompany the settlers before the forced evacuation and, as such, were less of an "enemy" to those on the verge of evacuation. As my colleague Lior Rosenberg and I discovered, there were many local leaders who, whether they opposed the evacuation or not, did nonetheless invest in the offering of services to the evacuees. Thus we found the head social worker and his staff caringly serving the settlers on their way out, in total opposition to what was considered politically correct and had been sanctioned as such. In addition, rabbis and their families, along with religious social workers went from house to house to support the evacuees who were feeling helpless and abandoned in the weeks leading up to the evacuation. They also knew how to restrain some youths who had intentionally joined the settlers prior to the evacuation in order to protest against it. All this made the evacuation and the resettlement more peaceful.

As the literature shows, despite the fact that forced evacuations occur in many parts of the world, almost nothing or very little has been written about how to accompany its injured parties, its "victims". This was different here, and that was perhaps because as researchers we belonged to a society which had had such a terrible history related to expulsion, and thus we were more than ready to learn about effective modes of accompanying and supporting those who were to be evicted.

Be that as it may, politically forced evacuations can also provide new opportunities for those affected. Thus, as a social worker and as someone seeking opportunities to support victims of this kind of collective violence, I am confident that studies of forced evacuations of the past which would have used the "learning from success" ideas if not methodology, could have been of benefit for evacuees in the future. This could have been furthered, for instance, by enabling them to benefit from different kinds of reciprocity on their way and which could have made the evacuation easier for them. Indeed, like the committed volunteers who had come there and were grateful for having been enabled to assist the evacuees, the evacuees were grateful for the volunteers' generosity and tenderness.[7]

In retrospect I may say that in the course of this post-evacuation, I, for the first time, could more clearly understand the idea of reciprocity to which we shall return in Section V.

As this became clearer and clearer, it enabled us to discern the distinct differences between the two evacuations and what they had in common. The distinct difference was that the first evacuation had been imposed on both the evacuees and the Israeli society and the second one had been supported by the society to which the evacuees also belonged, though not necessarily by the majority of either. What we discovered in the second evacuation was that the evacuees tended to consent to the evacuation, and they did not have feelings of betrayal and indignation directed at those who, by being with them, may have sanctioned it.

What could be learned from this is that in the course of the Sinai evacuation there was at best a sense of collective solidarity among those being evacuated. What they had to undergo remained puzzling to them and thus in their way of addressing it there was much formality, preoccupation with politics and with little space left for personal concern, but even an over-emphasis on "getting it over".

By contrast, in the second evacuation, while the ones to be evacuated were concerned about what was to come, those in charge of what was happening tended to be both caring and immersed in performing their duty as those responsible for the evacuation. Both those who were clearly evacuees and those in charge of evacuating them felt committed to acting together and, at the same time, to continuing their common protest. This enabled the ones to accompany and the others to be accompanied, which highlighted what was needed under these circumstances.

## 6. "TO BE A 'GOOD ENOUGH' PARENT": HOW NURSES IN WELL-BABY CENTERS IN ISRAEL IMPLEMENT A LEARNING PROGRAM ADDRESSING EARLY CHILDHOOD NEGLECT IF NOT ABUSE (ROSENFELD, 2010)[8]

This section expands upon my initial five years of work with nurses (Rosenfeld and Levy, 1997) in Well-Baby Centers in Jerusalem, originating in the early 1950s. Building on that earlier exploratory study, the present project was started about twenty years ago with the explicit goal of introducing the idea and the concept of "Good Enough Parenting" into the Well-Baby Centers in Israel. From its beginnings, the conception was that it would be an "ongoing" program, in line with its mission, as it is related to the heart of what "good enough" parenting is all about. The conception emerged without having been clearly planned or "spelled out". This may not have been entirely by choice, since the program is like the pattern established between parents and children from the beginning of their "joint venture". What seems particularly appropriate and relevant in this program is that it is in line with the developmental ideas related to "good-enough parenting", rather than paying attention to "problem solving", like eating difficulties or sleeping disorders. By not addressing these latter problems we were able to introduce the "learning from success" methodology that calls for reflection-based learning. To do so accords with the exploration of actions that had been effective in the past and can, as such, provide a basis for introducing ideas for use in the present and thus for the future. In turn, this was enabled by the avoidance of seeing this work as based on moving beyond crises. This permitted the work of nurses and families to jointly accompany the development of the relations between parents and children at the beginning of life. It also offered them an introduction to "learning from success", which was bound to further their capacity of being "good enough" (Winnicott, 1953). In addition, "learning from success" enabled them to pave their own way for "ongoing learning", which is likely to fashion their becoming and being "good enough".

I had much of this in mind twenty years ago when I initiated the program together with the (at the time) Head of Well-Baby Centers, the late Bat-Sheva Levy. It began with two-to-three hour learning sessions twice a month with the nurses in Bet-Shemesh, a small town near Jerusalem. As it turned out, those who were in charge of the dissemination of the program were not the regional supervisors, who attended only a few of these sessions. Its disseminators were nurses from different nearby centers who used to attend all or most meetings and thus became partners to learning and who took it upon themselves to be the self-appointed disseminators of the program.

These learning sessions provided the nurses with the basis for our work with the local head nurses, who had become the promoters of the program vis-à-vis the rotating heads of the Well-Baby Center Services. At our monthly meetings, the nurses were asked to present situations where they had "given up" on a family or parent, i.e. on situations that troubled the nurse and for which she felt she had no solution. While initially the nurses called such a situation a "defeat", one of the achievements of the program was their reframing the event and seeing it as an "impasse". This meant it was no longer seen as somebody's failure and then giving up on her/him. Whether the "impasse" was between the parent and the child or between the parent and the nurse, such "impasses" referred either to parents whose children were in trouble or those who did not take advantage of the services offered, either by not coming to see the nurse, by not following up the nurse's advice or even by being at loggerheads with her.

To address these impasses, the program suggested that nurses think of ways to encourage and enable parents to feel being "good enough" rather than spending time searching for explanations for their difficulties, let alone their failures as parents. Based on the assumption that being "good enough" is what might enable infants and children to develop and use their own inborn capacities required us to assist the nurses to stay attuned to what was happening and to involve *all* partners as "resources" of the program: the children; the parents; the nurses; social agencies; the local welfare department; and all other stakeholders. With regard to each and every stakeholder, the nurses sought to encourage them to find their own way to mobilize resources which could be of benefit to the child and its family, i.e. to encourage and not to confront. Accordingly, it was often suggested that an impasse between a nurse and a mother reflected an impasse between the mother and her child. In light of this suggestion, nurses who participated in the program were encouraged to suggest alternative modes of intervening, which facilitated acting with a sense of partnership between the nurse and the mother and facilitated the move beyond the "impasse" between them. Nurses were asked to gather as much information as possible and then to jointly formulate and consider which alternative actions might be employed to resolve the situation. As I came to understand later, once we had developed the ideas of "learning from success", it turned out that interventions with a focus on ongoing and reflection-based deliberations, i.e. on actual actions rather than on explanations, were the most relevant ones.

Today I would say we have learned to do so in the course of mastering the "learning from success" approach. To do so meant not to focus on explanations of behavior, i.e. diverting one's attention from what is to be done, and not to explain the reasons for doing so, which could only divert one from one's primary commitment to find ways of acting effectively.

Two stories follow which show how, in the context of our program and with the support of their colleagues, two nurses used reflection-based learning (Schön, 1983) generated by their learning group. The stories show how two extremely endangered infants and their overwhelmed mothers were helped to move beyond an impasse between a mother and her child, or between a mother and a nurse, and enabled to move beyond their reciprocal exclusion.

## First Story: When a nurse had to abandon an abandoned pregnant mother of four children

The first is a story of a pregnant, almost toothless and deaf woman, who at the time of this event was the mother of four children; clearly "excluded" family. She was from a low socio-economic background, had been diagnosed as schizophrenic, and was married to a man who was chronically unemployed. The family did not receive regular social services from the authorities. The mother had suffered from post-partum depression after one of the previous births, and now reported loneliness and longing for her family of origin, who lived far away. When she was first seen by the nurse, the mother, who had never previously met the nurse, told her that she was her only friend and asked her to lend her fifty shekels which the nurse did not do. However, she did invite the mother to return the next day. The mother did not return.

As her due date grew closer, the mother returned to the center and reported feeling afraid of the forthcoming birth. When the nurse asked her how she might be of help, the mother asked, "Could you come and hold my hand during the birth?" The nurse said that she could not help her at the birth, but that she would attempt to find her someone else, which, however, she was not able to do in the end. Eventually, while the mother's husband looked after the other children, one of her children's teachers held her hand during the birth and in this way supported her. When, for her own reasons, the nurse moved to another center, the mother felt abandoned. But then, because of the mother's past experience with depression, the nurse requested and received her supervisor's agreement to visit the mother after the birth together with the mother's new nurse.

Up to this point, the nurse concerned had not shared all this at the monthly meetings with her colleagues. Eventually, when she did, the nurse voiced her wish to assist the children of this woman who were about to be taken away, and she asked the advice of the nurses in their learning group. Several opinions were voiced:

a. The woman seems manipulative.
b. Her manipulative personality seems to actually facilitate her being effectively resourceful.
c. The nurse ought to remain in regular contact with the mother's social workers, to share with them any changes in the mother's predicament.
d. If she intended to see the children, it had to be through contact with the mother.

At the next meeting, we heard that when the nurse formally transferred the care to the new nurse, the children and the mother expressed sincere gratitude for the help she had given them. It turned out that in the aftermath of this work, the nurse who took over this family was able to work effectively for the well-being of this formerly seriously underserved mother and her family.

## Second Story: On the self-emancipation of a nurse and a mother, both from the same Bedouin village.[9]

In a Bedouin village in the remote south of the country, the wife of an unemployed twenty-eight-year-old battering father who appeared disinterested in both his 2 ½ year-old child and his six-month-old child, came into a Well-Baby Center. When the baby cried, the mother didn't hug him, made no eye-contact with him, and the baby's records show that he had failed to gain weight.

When the nurse and the mother—both Bedouins from the same village— had previously come to the center, the mother scarcely spoke, and only reported quietly that she felt lonely and scared. She told the nurse that she didn't trust her, and it transpired that from where the mother lived, she felt alienated from her own family and her neighbors. She also experienced regular intimidation at the hands of the battering husband and his controlling mother, and thus was left without any sources of support.

During our meetings, the nurse's colleagues simply suggested that she should visit the woman a few times even though she was reluctant to do so since she and the mother lived in the same village and knew each other. The nurses suggested that she should use her identity as a "nurse" and not as a neighbor. When the nurse proceeded to do so, after a few visits the situation changed radically. It changed so much so that the nurse dared to urge the mother to find her own voice and to fight for her rights. That included not allowing herself to be beaten by her husband, and telling her own family about her situation. When she did so, she indeed became less isolated. At this stage the nurse also helped the mother to secure part-time childcare, to find work and also to join a women's support group in her village.

Upon reflection, we learned from when one of the nurses, who had read Winnicott and Bowlby, expressed the thought that the setting of this mother's family was not so different from that of her nurse. Whereupon, it dawned on the nurse who was living in the same village that this mother had the same rights in her family as the nurse had in hers. This then enabled her to look at this mother differently, i.e. not as a seemingly hopeless and resource-less person. Then, when the nurse started to talk to her with respect, the mother expressed her wish to connect with other mothers and thus to join other communal services. Throughout this time, the mother's situation at home continued to improve. This transformation happened in light of the support she was receiving from the nurse who talked to her and for her did, for the first time as someone who too had the same rights as any Bedouin mother. It, as that, had enabled her to see that she had the same rights and the same capacity to claim her rights as others had. When the nurse told this to her colleagues in the "Good Enough Parent" workshop, they laughed and celebrated her own and the mother's "emancipatory knowledge". Quite often nurses who live in patriarchal, traditional communities like this one need the support of their peers to take steps towards their own, and then to their client's, emancipation.

## Some of the Successes and Achievements of the "Good Enough Parent" Program

In the absence of any formal evaluation of the "Good Enough Parent Program" and reflecting on the "Learning from Success" approach to which the nurses had been exposed, I shall first consider some of the achievements of the program and then follow them with a short description of how the program is currently being introduced in other centers.

1. The program is by now spreading to more and more centers and thus it actually operates amongst the more peripheral populations such as Arabs and Bedouins, who have few other services at their disposal. The nurses there are becoming increasingly autonomous without wanting to train for it formally.

2. "The 'good enough' parent" approach is becoming increasingly universal, addressing more and more mothers and children, and not just those with extreme disabilities. The program overcomes the counterproductive tendency

to have nurses become specialists in one or another area of infant care, rather than as a nurse who serves all families, not according to her specialization or thus not by referring the mother to one or another distinct special sphere of service offered by the nurses of the centers.

3. The increasing and evidently unique contribution and innovative developments of the Well-Baby Centers as a public health service for children has had one additional and unforeseen effect. It has, to some extent, prevented the introduction of a clinical approach rather than maintaining the clear public health orientation which these centers always clearly had.

4. The inspectorate of the center, who initially had been quite skeptical about the relevance of the program, has become more and more supportive. However, the program is not yet a formal part of the centers and it was decided to continue introducing it in the same informal way as was done in the past. For example, by letting the concern for "good enough" parenthood emerge in the course of the common work of the nurses without it having been formally introduced.

5. In both districts where the program operates, the number of nurses who participated in this program has increased and nurses who have participated in it over time have initiated introducing it to a wider circle of nurses, who in turn have introduced it to more and more centers and districts.

6. Finally, because of the introduction of the "learning from success" approach in Well-Baby Centers, other services, such as education and welfare centers, have gained interest in the approach and are gradually becoming partners.

As I have often learned, the chances of a program being successful are greater when its structure and way of functioning are related to and relevant to its content, as this case demonstrates. Therefore, in closing, I would say that there is one important lesson to be learned from "learning from success". It is that of introducing a new and seminal concept like "to be a 'good enough' parent" into a well-established service like Well-Baby Centers in Israel and to ensure its dissemination over time, seems to be possible given two factors: *first*, that it be introduced by a trusted outsider; and *second*, that the central idea of being a "good-enough parent" should not be seen as obvious, but one that has to be internalized and cannot be simply taught. Consequently, the program of being a "good-enough parent" needed to be gradually introduced, and "digested" over time. This process is something only a well-disposed, caring and non-hierarchical authority can support. It is similar to wanting one's daughter to be a caring mother. There too it is best neither to instruct nor to criticize her but to support her caringly, tolerantly and over time. And this is what, in the course of their work, those responsible for the Well-Baby Centers have been able to do gradually and informally.

## The Contribution of the "Learning From Success" Method

Towards the end of this section, it may be well to consider how one might introduce the "learning from success" method and, in its wake, "ongoing learning" in human services in Israel and beyond it.

"Learning from Success", which is based on the ideas of "positive deviance", has been employed in recent years by the "Unit for Learning from Success and for Ongoing Learning in Human Services[10]", of the Myers-JDC-Brookdale Institute in several fields: education; social welfare; the right to work (Wisconsin) Program; and lately the work of ATD Fourth World Movement. What has been documented here is how to induce nurses to study their own past successes with parents, to present how they had achieved this success, by putting it in actionable terms, and then as a basis for becoming "ongoing learners" both as individuals and within their collegiate system. This mode of operation was adapted to the Well-Baby Centers since the ideas related to being a "good enough" parent were introduced. Thus just by utilizing the learning culture of the Well-Baby Center system, lectures and courses from the outside, may not always be in tune with what is at the heart of the mission of the work of the nurses.

To end with a personal epilogue, I would say that the repeated accounts I had heard in my family about the contribution of nurses to me during the first six weeks of my life in the hospital (see 1.1), may well have contributed to my firm loyalty and passion for my work with the nurses of Well-Baby Centers in Israel. Irrespective of this, I believe that what is unique in this program is that it enabled these nurses to contribute to parents at the beginning of their parenting journeys, by introducing the "good enough parents" approach. This being there as a formally "sanctioned" program, it could become "self- disseminating" and may thus have been adopted in the course of their work and their mission, without it having been named "the science of caring" (Watson 1979).

## 7. "OUT FROM UNDER": A FIRST STUDY ON "LEARNING FROM THE SUCCESS OF ORGANIZATIONS SERVING SOCIALLY DEPRIVED FAMILIES IN ISRAEL" (ROSENFELD, 1992) (ROSENFELD, SCHÖN AND SYKES, 1995)

For many years I was unable to find a way to introduce social workers and others who work with and for the benefit of socially deprived families in Israel to the methods of ATD—the Fourth World Movement. This difficulty was largely due to the differences between the setting of the Israeli and other organizations in charge of welfare, and that of ATD Fourth World Movement. While the former operate as organizations within the context of the state or local authorities and/or the nonprofit sector, the latter work not as members of an organization but of a worldwide movement, and each as a permanent volunteer corps.

Then, one day in the late eighties, I again met Donald Schön, a professor at M.I.T. who used to visit Israel once or twice a year. I immediately told him that I would like to engage him in learning with us about the successes of social workers working with socially deprived families in Israel. Thereupon, in his perceptive and charming manner, he asked me, "Why not learn from failure?" Without any hesitation, I responded, "If you want to learn from failure, do so with someone else, because there are so few successes and so many failures." It was that conversation which provided the "click" between us. Together with this erudite and inventive man of the world, I and others in Israel again followed in the footsteps of Chris Argyris, "not to explain the world but to change it"[11].

On the basis of this conversation, I introduced Donald Schön to Jack Habib, the then Head of the Joint Distribution Committee, and later Head of the Myers-JDC-Brookdale Institute. It was agreed that together we would plan and initiate a seminar at which we would present examples and then records of successful programs for deprived families in Israel.

At that point I recruited into this venture the unforgettable, late Ora Namir, a student of mine and then my colleague, who had written a groundbreaking story of her work with the "Jaffe Family" (Namir, 1999). Ora's work was written about when she was seventeen years old. It was an account of her work with a family that was about to have nine of their children taken away and placed in foster care. Because of Ora's authentic and powerful work, the separation of the children from their parents did not occur. There is one memorable account of Ora's work with the children. She recounts how one day, as she and the nine children were walking through the streets of Jerusalem, a group of youngsters teased them by calling them names including *"aniyiim"*, which means "poor people" in Hebrew. Ora's response was to encourage the Jaffe children to use the same melody and call their tormenters in return, "bney-zonot", which means "sons of prostitutes" in Hebrew. To respond in this manner to the sneering youths, who had made fun of the extremely impoverished children, gave the Jaffe children a sense of also having a voice. It cancelled out the cruel teasing, which reduced the poor children to despised objects. Ora also inspired and encouraged the father of the children, then an unemployed tailor, to sew his children costumes for Purim[12] enabling him to do something for his children that he was able to do. These are only two examples of Ora's unusual capacity for being actively attuned to a family excluded from Israeli society, one of those who rarely are seen and addressed. I take this opportunity to pay tribute to this extraordinarily gifted and intelligent colleague and friend who died all too early, several years ago.

It was Ora Namir who, together with Israel Sykes, one of the partners of this work, collected eight accounts of successful interventions by social workers and others who worked with seriously socially and economically deprived families and their children. These and other stories became the material we used at a first learning seminar in 1993, facilitated by Don Schön and myself. During those unforgettable three days we learned from and with Don about "Reflection In- and On- Action", as a tool for discerning "actionable knowledge", which refers to actions that make a difference to the lives of families and others (Schön, 1979, 1987, 1991). The quest for such knowledge helped us identify and extract, from the eight accounts, thirteen common "Principles of Action", which had contributed to these families, and which could be introduced into the repertoire of actions to be employed as needed to help families in the future. The primary principle was the fact that those who had initiated and continued with these programs were those who had been touched by the tenderness of these families.[13] Another one was their readiness to continue serving these families who had persistently pursued them to receive the help they needed.

Based on this learning, three of us wrote a Hebrew and English text which we named, "Out from Under" (Rosenfeld, Schön and Sykes, 1995), a name that suggested what needed to be done in order to succeed in working with severely socially deprived families and their children in order to enable them to move beyond their exclusion. I may add here that this seminar was the first of several in which the participants spelled out and described in actionable language how to help other similarly un(der)served families.

Surprisingly, when we presented and shared these thirteen Principles of Actions with other social workers, they tended to respond with, "We do this anyway". Their saying so was striking because it highlighted that many, if not most, of the modes of interventions or the crafts which social workers employ are based on that tacit knowledge which they had knowingly acquired from what had worked in the past or learned from past successes, and not, for example, on actions derived from theories.

In the aftermath of this seminar and the publication of our book, we facilitated a series of seminars and subsequent publications that presented the potential power of "Learning from Success" tools. We offered our findings in "actionable terms" in Israel and beyond and at formal presentations we did so by amending the version of the song "Anything you can do I can do better", into: "Anything I can do, you can do too." This reflects how, when it comes to disseminating findings derived from the learning from success method, it could not have come about without the availability and generosity of those who had offered service to the populations they served. As outlined in Parts V and VI, in the course of struggling to find effective modes of addressing the previously "un(der)served" and creating a sense of ownership of their own work, we highlighted the importance of our findings not as our own personal possession but as "knowledge-for-action" that is to be handed over to others (Rosenfeld, 1987).

At this point I want to acknowledge my own, and on behalf of many others, deep gratitude to and appreciation of the late Donald Schön, who personified freedom of thought as a basis for introducing "reflection on/in action" and as a primary source for identifying those practices in social work. What is unique about this reflection-based approach is that it first of all legitimizes freeing oneself from preconceived ideas and theories as sources of practice, and that by doing so one is free to focus on the actionable knowledge derived from one's own experience in the course of one's work. Doing things in this way implies looking for actions which have made the difference rather than following theories to be applied. It was thanks to Don Schön that the ideas connected with "Learning from Success" and "Reflective Practice" were introduced while setting up the Unit of Learning from Success and Ongoing Learning in Human Services at the Myers-JDC-Brookdale Institute in Israel. It is my work in this Institute which has enabled me to sponsor different projects in which services benefit from what "Learning from Success" had to offer in the fields of social welfare, education, or health in Israel and beyond it. Doing so did not just require the "unearthing" of "tacit knowledge" in different settings and countries, but also in finding the commonalities across these settings and societies. It provides a common ground for serving the "un(der)served in our midst" wherever they may be. At the same time, it introduced a sense of universality as well as the idea of their commonalities, and it freed each of them from adhering to an isolating sense of uniqueness and thus from their actual isolation. Therefore, this showed their belonging to what ATD considers that the lives of "people living in poverty" should be like.

Creating such universality is of great importance for the work of ATD Fourth World Movement, which addresses the needs of the poorest of the poor in many societies. Such a creation has also enabled and encouraged this incredibly modest and resourceful movement to share effective modes of their work with other organizations and movements (see part VI). In similar veins, with our help, it has also initiated introducing and training for Learning from Success in different fields of work with other people who had been seriously isolated, and to see each of them as collectives and not just as individuals.

## NOTES

1. Chris Argyris to Jona Rosenfeld in a private conversation, circa 1964.
2. Rosenfeld and Rosenstein (1973); Rosenfeld, Rosenstein and Raab (1973).
3. I thank Bilha Manheim, one of our partners in that enterprise, for reviewing and editing this section, almost 50 years later.

4. I thank Amilia Aviel-Dinai for her thoughtful comments on the version of this section which came 45 years later.

5. Moses, Hrushovsky-Moses, Rosenfeld and Beumel (1985).

6. Jerusalem Quarterly, 22. Fall 1984.

7. In this connection we refer to Part IV.4 where some of those who had suffered from crisis when their houses had burned down had benefitted from this undesirable event.

8. Based on a paper presented at the ACWA Conference on Early Intervention and Family Support Session, Sydney, August 3, 2010.

9. Bedouins are Israeli citizens, who are a minority within the Arab minority. In recent years, they have received increased attention, both from the media and government.

10. See Appendix II.

11. Chris Argyris in a conversation with Jona Rosenfeld in the 1990's.

12. Purim is the festival which showcases Queen Esther of the Bible and which is celebrated by dressing up in costume.

13. It is striking that totally independently, a study of families living in extreme poverty and exclusion of the Fourth World Movement also found that it was the tenderness of the families that had recruited service organizations to attend to them (see VI.4).

*Part V*

# Moving beyond Exclusion Means Initiating and Introducing Reciprocity

## 1. ON THE MOVE FROM EXCLUSION TO RECIPROCITY AND HOW TO FACILITATE IT

The primary theme of this book is the move from exclusion to the initiation of reciprocity and of how to bring it about. Exclusions mean states of being with little or no social or human interaction or transactions with others. The exclusions to which we refer here tend to be of social origin, be it their having been created by individuals or collectives, and for or by political, social and economic systems. The ways beyond exclusions occur in the wake of introducing on reciprocity-based transactions initiated and enabled by any other. Such transactions are bound to have an impact on the lives of individuals and collectives who live in exclusion, whose move beyond exclusion occurs when anyone, knowingly or not, has become both a benefactor, who has contributed to the other, and a beneficiary of that other's contribution. This applies to the excluded and to those who initiated or participated in the initiation of reciprocity in the course of their encounters. Thus reciprocity is not only the goal but also a formative means for introducing the way to move beyond exclusion, and beyond the absence of interactions and transactions between the excluded and those who have the resources which they need. And, moreover, in most of these exclusions, the "actual" act of introducing—at times *re*introducing—reciprocity occurs when reciprocity is at its lowest. This implies that those who come to use and benefit from reciprocity most are those who had been least likely to break away from extreme exclusion, which the reciprocity had introduced right from the beginning of their encounter with the other. In this way those who are most disconnected and most excluded are encouraged not to remain anonymous, not to remain passive, and in this manner then, possibly, have the chance to move beyond exclusion towards reciprocity (Douglas, 2007).

These understandings have become clearer to me in the course of my experience with "learning from success" and again while writing this book. I have become increasingly aware of the different dimensions of reciprocity for each of the stakeholders, for the excluded on the one hand, for those having assumed the role of initiating it on the other. Anybody who, by becoming ready and actively involved in doing whatever is needed to act as a beneficiary of the "un(der) served", i.e. the excluded, both assume the role of stakeholder in that enterprise. Hence both those who initiated and furthered the former's moving beyond exclusion, i.e. their initiating the introduction of reciprocity to those who are clearly the former's benefactors, but also their beneficiaries, those who owe them their gratitude, irrespective of whether they show it or not.

Beyond this and as can be seen in the context of this book, whilst becoming acquainted with the aggregate of experiences of this learning, and by engaging in reflective learning, and this may also make it possible to identify the three Methods of Learning from Success (see Appendix III), which equips one to learn.

Furthermore, in the course of learning from these, on retrospection-based encounters, when participants or stakeholders learn with and from each other, it is bound to dawn on each of the participants that each has been of benefit to the other. Once one is ready and equipped to do so, the stage is set for "ongoing learning" and for disseminating both learning from success and the nature of the yields of this learning.

We shall not address here what may be common to the actions employed, including the underlying principles of action for identifying the capacities required for initiating moves beyond exclusion towards reciprocity, which could inevitably serve as guidelines for developing the knowledge required for furthering this practice as Krumer-Nevo (2005) has done.

Developing this knowledge is a challenge for the future and requires seeking, finding and initiating reciprocity-based learning and especially in contexts and settings committed to serving the un(der)served in our midst. This learning, in turn, is also relevant for introducing ongoing learning related to other, different kinds of exclusion. Indeed, only on the basis of collecting an aggregate of such examples may one understand that this lies at the heart of reciprocity-based learning and action, this for the benefit of the emergence beyond extreme exclusion, in ways that include identifying the numerous stakeholders involved in it (Barzilai, Rosenfeld and Fadida-Peleg, 2014).

## 2. ON THE LEARNING OF PRACTICES THAT FACILITATE THE MOVE FROM EXCLUSION TO RECIPROCITY

For a wide variety of reasons there are few practices based on academic knowledge available for initiating the move from exclusion to reciprocity (Krumer-Nevo, 2005). With this in mind, we shall now address the three origins of factors that initiate and pave the way for reflective learning on what the move from exclusion to reciprocity of the under-served in our midst is based:

1. *Personal abilities,* which include generosity and the ability to be partners in this enterprise.
2. *Settings* that enable reflective learning among multiple stakeholders.
3. The *three methods of learning* from success as a means for ongoing learning.

### 1. *Personal abilities,* which include generosity and readiness to be partners in reflective learning enterprises

Those engaging in this kind of learning need to possess or gradually acquire the quality of *generosity*—"the fellow feeling of and for the other's pleasure" (Smith, 1759). Without this, it seems unlikely that anyone can rise to the challenge of engaging in the journey of initiating, let alone introducing reciprocity where exclusion existed. Generosity, in the widest sense of the word, is called for whenever engaging in what is relevant for retrospective learning. As such, it is necessary for reaping the benefits of this learning, for thus becoming part of the lives of the formerly-excluded and "for contributing to the other's pleasure", as in the examples to follow. Stakeholders who have succeeded in doing so possess or have acquired the generosity needed for being or becoming and thus remaining *partners*, i.e. stakeholders or colleagues for this learning throughout the move from exclusion to reciprocity. This, for instance, is in contrast to learning that is mainly "results oriented", which bars one from becoming a learning partner in the kinds of non-hierarchical settings as the ones which reflective learning from success calls for.

### 2. *Settings* that enable "reflective learning" among multiple shareholders

Ensuring "reflective learning" both individually and among multiple stakeholders can only occur in settings where there is an awareness that organizational hierarchy may impede the search for effective actions. Effective actions, in turn, require that the excluded and any of their other relevant, actual or potential partners do not drop out and that they contribute as partners in initiating reciprocal and joint learning and are able and willing to engage in furthering learning ventures. The latter needs settings with the ethos of collective learning, and not of authority and hierarchy. What this collective ethos furthers is that it accepts that the delegation of roles is determined by the quest for ongoing joint, and on reflection-based collective learning. This is what is relevant for the emergence from exclusion and for creating opportunities for on joint reflection-based learning, without which both ongoing joint learning and the move towards reciprocity cannot happen.

## 3. The Three "Methods of Learning from Success" (see Appendix III)

The final prerequisite for facilitating these processes is systematic employment of the three methods of learning from success developed by The Unit of Learning from Success. The *first* method focuses on retrospection-based identification and recording the actions related to the moves beyond exclusion, the other two are there to maintain and pave the way for doing so. All three methods equip one to introduce the processes of learning from success, not only systematically, but also to ensure the applicability of what has been learned. This furthers what is vested in the pursuit of reflective learning aimed at providing information on what actions might enable one to emerge from exclusion to reciprocity.

*The First Method — The Retrospective Method —*
*Learning from Past Success.*

Doing so enables one to identify the actions which brought about the success in the past and thus for the present and future.

*The Second Method — The Prospective Method —*
*Learning with and from a Learning Question or Quest.*

This in order to formulate actions and principles of action on the basis of actionable past experiences, if not expertise, for immediate use.

*The Third Method — The Reflective Method —*
*Learning on Learning from and for Actions.*

The aim of this method (and it is the one still being developed) is to introduce effective learning, relevant to the themes of this book.

With this in mind, in the next part (VI), we describe how much investment and time may be required for the long-term accompaniment which may be necessary to enable one person who was exposed to the Holocaust to move from his exclusion to living a truly on reciprocity-based life.

It is hoped that the section provides readers with a sense of what is required to set the stage for the move from exclusion to the initiation of reciprocity of one's life story which, without following any methodology, does enable the move from impasse and exclusion to a life of reciprocity.

# VI

# The Evolving of Reciprocity: The Long Journey of Chaim Who Survived the Holocaust at the Age of Three

Written with Chaim

This point in the book may be the place to relate one of the most important experiences in my career if not life. It is the story of Chaim (his real name), a boy from the Holocaust whom I first, encountered as a young social worker in the early 50's. Already on this occasion it came as a (never-ending) surprise to learn what, in today's language, "the move beyond exclusion" represents. What is relevant and pleasing about this idea is that it has roots in where I came from, in what I studied and in how I practiced what I believed in from the beginning, and this with the help of so many extraordinary colleagues. After being with Chaim for so many years, I became someone who believes that moving beyond where one has come from is possible. This happens when one, like him, is accompanied over time on the search for ways beyond one's past.

I met Chaim when he was twelve years old and a member of a children's group run by unusually caring and generous staff, in a kibbutz. He was brought by one of his concerned counselors to the mental health clinic in Jerusalem in which I worked as a social worker. He came there because he was repeatedly wetting his bed at night. Chaim was a very good-looking youngster, very intelligent but also somewhat evasive, and consequently he refused to come to work with me on his bedwetting.

All I knew about him at the time was that he was born in the late 30's in Poland and when he was three-and-a-half years old his parents together with an aunt and an uncle went to live in an underground shelter. He remained there for about a year and a half and, just one week before the end of the war, his parents went off to get food for him and never returned. Some Poles had turned them over to the Germans. From there on he remained with his aunt and uncle, the ones whose child had been killed at the beginning of the holocaust.

As he came to see me irregularly, I told him that if he would not come to therapy, being parentless, all I could do was to turn to the only "parents" he had—the heads of Youth Aliya, the Immigrant and Children's Youth Organization to which he belonged. I told him that I would tell them that unless he came for treatment they, as the only parents he had, should send him to a children's home from which he could not abscond and where he would get the treatment he needed. After all, he had no other parents and I would do all I could for him to receive the help needed in order to stop him wetting his bed. To my great surprise, he started to come regularly and after a few weeks, during which we talked about some of the events and the horrors of his life during the Holocaust, he stopped wetting his bed.

At that point, he asked me to come and see him play basketball, which I did, and many years later I read what he had written in an account of his life: "When I was 12 years old Jona Rosenfeld came to see me play basketball and that was the first time anyone had seen me."

Today I see this as the initiation of reciprocity, by acknowledging that at some time there can be an "other" who saw one.

For the next two years he came to see me once a week and gradually told me his life-story and never again about his bedwetting. He told me how, when he was three years old, his parents had tried to place him in a Polish family next to their shelter in order to save him and how he, by himself, had found his way back from there. He also mentioned how, once he had found his aunt who had lost her way he, then also three years old, showed her how to return to the shelter and thus saved her life. He also repeatedly mentioned that in the underground shelter, whenever he cried, his mother would force a cushion over his face so that the Poles and Germans would not discover them.

Later he also told me that when, at the end of the war, their son was born and this after their first-born daughter had died during the war, his aunt and uncle had placed him in a children's home in Germany. He also told me that he had tried to escape from this children's home in Germany to return to his aunt and uncle who lived not too far away, by sneaking into the train by which they had brought him there. Another unforgettable story was how he had refused his aunt's and uncle's suggestion to emigrate to relatives in the

US and how instead at his insistence they entrusted him, a ten-year-old, to someone he had not known who took him to Israel.

During the first two years in Israel, he stayed with another maternal aunt and uncle who had come to Palestine before the Holocaust. There he did well in school, learned Hebrew well and forgot the languages he knew previously. Then, one day, he insisted on being placed in a children's home in a kibbutz. The explicit reason was that his uncle used to hit his children and that, as he told Chaim, he spared hitting him because he was a memorial of his parents, i.e. not his own person, and that that had hurt Chaim deeply and he insisted on leaving them.

In our weekly meetings at the mental health clinic, we played games together, talked about his current life and his previous one. All this was conducted in a very friendly way, and I scarcely remember any therapeutic interventions. But then, after two and a half years, I went to study abroad and suggested that we stay in touch. Before my final departure I brought him a stopwatch which I thought related to his having "stopped wetting the bed", to his interest in sports and also to my departure. During my six-year absence I wrote to him every so often and saw him during my one home visit. Since then we have not met in a clinic but consistently talked about his daily life, which included joining the army, learning to become a driving instructor, and eventually getting married (He invited me to the wedding). For some years they lived on the same kibbutz to which he had come and where his wife was born, which was a more or less "safe haven" for him until they decided to leave it.

At that time he had also gone to various therapists, none of whom appeared to have been of real help. And when they had not been of help to him after the 1973 Yom Kippur War, he came to see me from time to time to get help. He had undergone traumatic battle experiences on the Golan Heights, such as being under attack and under severe pressure, was and also felt neglected by his commanders.

During the early years he often asked me to adopt him, which I declined. But when he got older he went to study social work at the Hebrew University, where I worked and where I was the Dean of the School. As I was the head of the school, he wanted me to help him get accepted, but I did not. Upon his graduation I made a point to say in public that one of that year's graduates of the school had a story which was most unusual and that I was glad that he had become a social worker. Throughout these years we met in different places, including the school which his and our children attended. Then, about six years, ago he asked to come to me for therapy and he has attended once a week ever since. These have been regular meetings in my clinic, for which he does not pay. We have done very important work on his life-story and especially about his life during the Holocaust. We talked repeatedly about both his parents having abandoned him in order to get food, about his grandfather who, before the war, had played very memorable games with Chaim also related to his having snatched cubes of sugar from him. We talked about some of the fears he had and about the uncontrolled manner in which he shivered during our sessions which were partly related to his mother having put a cushion on his face when he used to cry in the shelter, so as not to be heard by the Germans. In time he also talked about his wounds, his trauma, which he connected to his parents leaving him without thinking that he was alone, his yearning for them, and his wondering who and how they had been. And yes, he felt that all he could do was to be their memorial.

At one point he also mentioned his fear of mountain climbing, until one day he half seriously said that his fear was that the mountains would drop him too. In time we also talked about his professional work, especially as a housefather of older people, many of them survivors of the Holocaust. Then before his retirement we talked at times about his plans for the future. It was then, for the first time, that he decided to learn play the mandolin, to take history courses, and to happily engage in other pursuits. His grandchildren became an ever-increasing topic in our discussions as were the members of his family in the past. Even after he burst into shivers when he felt clearly most upset, it became obvious that he felt more and more content with his life and also had more regular contact with friends. In addition, his wife and children had recently planned a journey to Poland. They went to see where he was born, where he lived in the underground shelter, and where he and his family had returned a few months after the end of the war, and where he had been a witness to an unforgettable massacre of Jews by the Poles at that time. He now looks much calmer, is more content with his life and more outspoken about what he is up to. When I asked him to tell me how he felt, he said without any hesitation that he is living a full life, and that he is much happier.

At the end of writing this I wondered if, and in what way, the elements of reciprocity in our contacts and relationship had contributed to his life. Whether it had or not, I believe that Chaim is one person with whom I learned what reciprocity is about. It was reflected in each of us having benefited from what we had done together for so many years. What I can say is that I discovered how I have benefited from our joint journey, from our extraordinary mutual trust, and from the idea that I have been able to be so loyal and of benefit to Chaim all these years, without thinking our joint venture would come to an end.

My relationship with Chaim had a number of components, each of which contributed to it in some way: our sense of friendship; our mutually respectful affinities; our so unusually non-intrusive intimacy. These have enabled us to work together to become who we are. Both of us, he the boy from the Holocaust, and I the social worker, the therapist, the friend, who have been able to remain partners, each owning his own authenticity for which each is more than grateful.

As we approach the end of this book, I would like to express both my gratitude to Chaim, who for about sixty years has provided me with the opportunity to be with him and to benefit in a way that enabled me to contribute to him—a very special person with an unusual story, and an unusual family. What is so significant here is that all of this was created in the aftermath of the Holocaust—the greatest travesty of our epoch and our lives.

Looking back, one element of my joint venture with Chaim became clear to me: it needed time, and readiness to accompany rather than to "cure" him; I needed to be available both for his daily life's events and for his life-story. This had to be done in a manner that was never intrusive and gave him the space for being and developing, without guiding him. More and more reciprocity emerged without having planned it and for each in his own way. Writing this together became an opening for him to talk about his pre-Holocaust good, early life with his parents, about whom he had never spoken before. In that way I gradually became his ever-changing "learning companion", with a more and more reciprocal personal relationship where I shared with him what was relevant for me in the context of our more regular meetings.

## POSTSCRIPT

He was not able to visit his father's town on his visit to Poland, and after reading this section, Chaim told me about a dream. The dream related to his having returned there to visit the town called Komarowsky. "When I was leaving it, I struggled not to do what I always did—not to be the heroic Samson and live the life of a memorial. At long last I had the power or the courage to weep as I had never done before." It is not by chance that when he was finally able to do so, he was also able to sense both his anger at his father's having left him and his yearning for him, by realizing what the word Komarowsky reminded him of: "to come karow", "karov" in Hebrew meaning to come close . . . to his early childhood.

# VII

# My Acquaintance with ATD* the Fourth World Movement: Where the Introduction of Reciprocity Is a Means for Moving Beyond Exclusion

### INTRODUCTION: ON INITIATING RECIPROCITY AND ONGOING LEARNING

On the face of it, the relation between reciprocity and exclusion does not appear obvious. However, when one considers what extreme exclusion is all about, it becomes clear that at the heart of exclusion lies a bare minimum of reciprocity. This is because when exclusion prevails reciprocal relationships, where participants can be both beneficiaries and benefactors, are unlikely to exist. What exists can, at best, be "mutuality" where, in line with the origin of the word, each borrows something from or lends something to the other. In contrast, when true reciprocity occurs, i.e. where it is not imposed, either morally or otherwise, each partner is affected by the other in ways that can generate change. Hence, exclusion is like in the city of Jericho, which "was tightly shut up . . . none went out and none came in"[1] . It is a situation with little chance for change, for personal emergence or for people having a crucial impact on one another. What characterizes exclusion is that mobility is minimal, stagnation and inactivity prevail and, consequently, there is bound to be a dearth of interactions, transactions and of opportunities for making choices. This characterization refers to a wide variety of exclusions, whether of one or more individuals or of one or more collectives.

Indeed, to deliberately set the stage for moving from exclusion to reciprocity does not just require the initiation of interactions, it requires on reciprocity-based transactions. These are transactions in which each player or stakeholder is at one and the same time both a beneficiary and a benefactor, something which the excluded in our midst have seldom experienced. Launching such transactions requires settings in which there is legitimacy for change and for ongoing learning rather than for rules and instructions.

To initiate such transactions requires an ongoing passion for serving the "excluded in our midst" and readiness to explore alternatives, to learn, to be surprised, to welcome what one had neither known nor thought about before. No less important is that those people who wish to initiate moves beyond exclusion have to be ready to be guided by what the un(der)served consider to be the ways to do so. To learn from and with them constitutes a first step towards "learning from success". In a complementary manner, moving beyond exclusion requires settings where a key element is a capacity and readiness to flatten hierarchy. This flattening is important because ongoing learning does not require individuals who have knowledge, but settings in which each stakeholder can contribute what he/she senses, learns, and remembers, often unknowingly. Doing so furthers the initiation and then introduction of reciprocity. This process necessitates the accompaniment of those we have called "learning companions", people equipped with the expertise of reflective practitioners (Schön, 1983).

To be a "learning companion" means to have the capacity to initiate and introduce on reciprocity-based transactions whenever they are needed. Indeed, learning companions are professionals but also include others who see themselves as partners initiating "give-and-take" modes of action in which each stakeholder is a beneficiary and a benefactor. In short, where each is a successful partner to in on-reciprocity-based transactions.

To do so requires the following:

- A readiness to discover how to move beyond the separateness or exclusion of the other.
- A capacity for seeing and naming that which separates people.
- A willingness to receive and accept from others what is useful and may be necessary.
- An ability to let go of any exclusion and to consciously initiate moves beyond it.

These conditions are likely to contribute to excluded individuals or groups by aiding them to cease acting or seeing themselves as victims of exclusion. The other stakeholders may thus also be enabled to cease viewing the excluded as victims and not as partners. The turning point in this process comes when partners are released from reciprocal exclusion on the one hand and engage in reciprocal transactions as a joint venture, on the other. For such a process to be successful, it often requires the presence of an outsider who accompanies the partners in their endeavor. In this context, it may be of importance to point out that in contrast to "reciprocity" being an obligation, here it is referred to as being a voluntary, even a desired and desirable experience and enterprise.

These understandings became increasingly evident to me over the course of working with and then writing two books with colleagues from ATD Fourth World Movement: "Emergence from Extreme Poverty" (Rosenfeld, 1989) and "Artisans of Democracy" (Rosenfeld and Tardieu, 2000). It was then that I realized for the first time how essential it is to get to know, learn, and then document the ways in which those who live in exclusion become able to move beyond it. It became evident that this process involves not only obtaining and using the necessary resources, but comes about by learning how those who have had such resources and known them, can offer them to those who need them. This is reflected in "Emergence from Extreme Poverty", that describes how members of ATD Fourth World Movement succeeded in aiding excluded families in moving beyond exclusion by engaging in reciprocal relations with them. "Artisans of Democracy" highlights how social organizations and other "stakeholders" engaged families living in extreme poverty to facilitate on reciprocity-based joint ventures with them. Both books describe how such transactions occur with and between families, organizations, and via give-and-take actions which allow each partner to contribute to the other, and then, to their common society.

Participating in this process knowingly, systematically and effectively constitutes what working towards reciprocity is all about. This is the case with regard to the move from exclusion to reciprocity of families and to other situations entailing mutual or even one-sided exclusion. What ATD Fourth World Movement does is just this: connecting and engaging families living in extreme poverty and the societies in which such poverty exists. To reiterate, the move from exclusion to reciprocity is a joint-venture in the sense that the partners are those who actually bring about the move beyond exclusion. The fact that exclusion is considered harmful to both the "excluders" and the excluded means that their respective well-being is intertwined and interdependent. In light of this, a "learning companion"[2] may well be able to take upon him/herself this task of systematically accompanying both of them towards or within their on reciprocity-based ventures.

It is at this point that I want to acknowledge and to express my gratitude for the contribution and the impact of the so fortunate encounter with the Fourth World Movement and not just to me personally and professionally but especially to my understanding of how essential it is to focus on reciprocity and on the so essential reciprocal contributions. This to both the erstwhile excluded—the "un(der)served" in our midst—and to those who in serving them, they can see themselves as joining them. It is that reciprocity which has paved the way to that optimistic and ongoing learning which is so essential for the excluded in our midst and their-our societies. To do so is at the heart of introducing the vision and mission of ATD beyond those who live in extreme poverty and exclusion.

It is in the connection with the above that it dawned on me that the initiation of reciprocity is the first step towards the initiation of the move beyond exclusion, there where there was a minimum of reciprocity.

## 1. IT'S PEOPLE LIVING IN POVERTY, NOT POVERTY

I cannot discern a clear origin of my interest in poverty, but I have always considered "serving the un(der)served in our midst" a high priority in my work as a social worker. As I mentioned earlier (Part III.3), the actual introduction of this theme into my life's work came about upon my return to Israel from studying in Chicago. It was then that I realized I could not "just" study poverty but that in order to understand and address issues that are relevant, what was needed was to study "people living in poverty" (Rosenfeld, 1962). As in other areas, this was part of my interest in people living in poverty and not in poverty as a phenomenon. To carry out my first study on the subject, it started with Eva Morris interviewing twenty-seven families living in poverty in their homes (Rosenfeld, Morris and Salzberger, 1969). One of the most noteworthy conclusions of that study was the discovery of how little we knew about the lives of people living amongst us in poverty, and especially those in extreme poverty.

As I explained earlier, probably out of my interest in individuals rather than in phenomena, I sought help from Yehuda Matras in finding objective criteria to differentiate between the lives of people actually living in extreme poverty—the "poorest in our midst"—and the lives of others in the entire population. To do so, we interviewed a sample of one thousand families about their "exigencies", i.e. objective indicators of need, and about what we came to call "predicaments" i.e. subjective indicators of need, like feeling healthy, having enough to eat, etc. (Rosenfeld, Salzberger and Matras, 1973). This was done in order to learn more about the specific conditions of life among those with the most exigencies i.e. those living in extreme poverty and who were chronically unseen. We compared their "predicaments" with those of families living in financial security. A fascinating finding has remained with me ever since. Using scales of four objective exigencies (income, housing, children and health), we learned that people living in the most extreme poverty reported the lowest numbers of "predicaments" and that people living in economic comfort reported the highest number of "predicaments". This showed that the subjective needs of the poorest families, when compared with other families, were absolutely minimal.

This finding led to my understanding that the low levels of expectations of the poorest families is a function of the almost non-existent resources at their disposal. Ever since doing this study, I have been trying to figure out what can be done to ensure that their low expectations do not continue to condemn people living in extreme poverty and exclusion to remain there. Also, that what they ought to be offered should be what they require in order to move beyond their own, or any socially-imposed, limitations. At that time I realized that they may require help with how to follow their dreams and overcome their limited aspirations. At this point I would like to mention that it was in 1970[3] that I presented this first-ever study of poverty in Israel to a meeting on poverty sponsored by the European Section of the United Nations which took place first in Bienne, Switzerland (and three years later in Oxford). It was then that I also had the opportunity to meet members of ATD Fourth World Movement for the first time.

## 2. HOW I GOT TO KNOW THE ATD FOURTH WORLD MOVEMENT: "THE MAN WHO WAS SHUSHED"

As I mentioned in part III.3, it is over forty years ago that, totally by chance, I became acquainted with the ATD Fourth World Movement. By chance, though as Louis Pasteur claimed: "In the field of observation, chance favors only the mind that is prepared." My encounter with this movement, which was founded more than 75 years ago to address the plight of families living in extreme poverty and exclusion, and which now operates in over thirty countries, occurred at the above-mentioned meeting convened by the European Section of the United Nations in Bienne, Switzerland. The meeting included about ten young researchers from different countries who, like me, had gathered to report on their studies of poverty in their respective countries. I reported on the first study which had been carried out on poverty in Israel, as I mentioned above. At the meeting, unexpectedly after each presentation, a Catholic priest, who turned out to be Père Joseph Wresinski, the founder of ATD Fourth World Movement, got up to say that he had grown up in poverty and that he wanted to say something about his own experiences with poverty. Whenever he got up he was shushed and, inevitably, had to sit down again, without anyone of the relatively young, budding researchers willing to hear his contribution.

I was upset by the way Père Joseph had been treated and when the session finished I went to join him for lunch. He was sitting with the Baroness Alwine de Vos van Steenwijk, later President of the International Movement

ATD Fourth World Movement, who had worked with the Red Cross in Holland during World War II and with Père Mario Borelli, an Italian priest who, at that time, was working with wayward boys in Naples. Almost before I had sat down, Père Joseph told me, totally out of the blue something in French that Madame de Vos had to translate: *"Families living in extreme poverty have something to contribute to the world."* I had no idea what he meant and it took me several decades of work and contemplation to truly understand what this, so very puzzling but meaningful statement, was all about. It was an idea which I, as a social worker and as a teacher of social work, had never thought about before. Since then this idea has never left me.

Two years later, in 1972, I met Père Joseph again, first at a UNESCO Conference in Oxford and then in Méry-sur-Oise, France, at the headquarters of ATD Fourth World Movement. Later on I told him that I had read "Lest Innocent Blood be Shed" by P. Hallie (1979) about Pastor Andre Trocmé and his wife Magda. It was they who, together with their family and village, saved 5,000 Jewish children from the Nazis. I told him that what the Trocmés had done for Jewish children in World War II was what ATD Fourth World Movement was doing for families living in extreme poverty. Trocmé had saved these children via a school in Chambon-sur-Lignon in the south of France, with the help of a German member of the Wehrmacht and the Quakers who had enabled them to cross the Pyrenees into Spain. Pastor Trocmé was killed by the Nazis and later trees in memory of him and his wife, his family and members of the village who had been killed were planted in the Holocaust Martyrs and Heroes Remembrance Authority, the Avenue of the Righteous of the Nations in Jerusalem.

At some point, he asked me to come with my family to Baillet-en-France in order to learn and formulate, together with members of ATD Fourth World Movement, the nature of the crafts they employ in their work with families living in extreme poverty.

Two summer seminars in 1981 became the first exposure of my wife Ruth, then 7-year-old No'a and 5-year-old Yael to ATD Fourth World Movement. We stayed in a motel near Baillet-en-France, near what is now called the International Joseph Wresinski Center and we went for our meals with them. Then and there also members of our family had been given the opportunity to meet more of the members of ATD Fourth World Movement who participated at the seminars and others, and to get a sense of what this so unusual movement was all about.

## 3. "EMERGENCE FROM EXTREME POVERTY": "SO YOU WANT TO KNOW ABOUT THE SUCCESSES OF THE FAMILIES"

The first of these seminars was in 1989, with about twelve members of its Permanent Volunteer Corps, including the late Mary Rabagliati from England and the late Bernadette Cornuau from France. Among its participants were Brigitte Jaboureck, who produced a story of work with a family living in extreme poverty and exclusion, as well as Bruno Dabout, a central member of the Movement, and Bruno Masurel whose role in the seminar we shall mention later. We all met for about five days from morning to evening in the presence of two or three translators, needed because of my limited French and the limited English of some of the participants.

Every morning, Père Joseph, the head of ATD Fourth World Movement, came by, spoke with our group and in the course of the day received feedback from Bernadette. The idea of the seminar was to explore the practices of the Volunteer Corps whose members had contributed to the well-being of the families with whom they worked. In fact, this was the first seminar which operated on the basis of the idea that we later named "learning from success", as an opportunity for spelling out the practices employed by the members of the Movement. It constituted what I later recognized as what Donald Schön called their "tacit knowledge", or their "theories in use", i.e. what they had actually done and that had an impact without their doing so knowingly.

The heart of "reflective learning" in and on action taken in the course of the seminar was revealed in response to specific questions posed to members of the Volunteer Corps, inviting them to spell out those actions which had contributed to the well-being of the families. For the first two days nobody managed to produce a story or event and extract from it what we later called "tactics and strategies producing successes." On the third day, when I had become somewhat desperate and thought my inadequate French was the cause of the impasse, I asked, somewhat impatiently, "Tell me about at least one success in your work with the families!" Suddenly Bruno Masurel, a tall, lively member of the Volunteer Corps from Marseille said, "So you want us to tell stories about the *successes* of families, not the successes of us members of the permanent Volunteer Corps!" With this, the participants finally produced the stories from which we all wanted to learn. It became clear that these were the actual actions of members of the Volunteer Corps for which we were looking. From then on, our emphasis was on how they had acted, without the need to provide any explanations or reasons for having done so. This was because to learn from success one needs to learn from the actions taken which brought the success about. It was the actions that provided a basis for repeating them in the present and for the future. The stories which followed provided the basis for the book on the seminar (Rosenfeld, 1989). It included the example of the work of Brigitte Jabourek with one particular family which wonderfully illustrated the unique mode in which members of ATD Fourth World Movement were acting in their work with these families. This was always shown with the emphasis on what they had done without any explanations.

The following week I attended an International Action Seminar of ATD Fourth World Movement where I learned more about how its members worked across the world. This helped me to put into words what had emerged during the first week and to get a glimpse of how this organization, nay movement, worked in other countries. This endeavor, I believe, set the stage for introducing the ideas of "learning from success" to those who attended that seminar.

There was one crucial insight that I gained from the memorable comment of Bruno Masurel. I realized that I had met people who did not think that what a family benefited from was what they, or others from the outside, had done. Whatever they did was not as significant as the unexpected benefits, i.e. the capacities of the families themselves. That was the first time I became fully aware of how patronizing my social work colleagues and I were. This became an understanding that has never left me since. It was this understanding that enabled me, for the first time, to appreciate that families living in poverty had, as ATD Fourth World Movement claimed, something to contribute to society. I had heard Permanent Volunteer Corps members saying just that again and again, but until then I had not understood that by not hearing these families I did not know what they needed. It was the same kind of "not hearing" that deprived society from benefiting from what the families had to contribute to it. From that day on I became better able to listen and to search more seriously for values, activities, and instances of hope, encouragement and dignity that these families contributed to society. In this connection, let me provide a recent example from my work on the Israeli Government's Committee on the eradication of poverty appointed in 2013. At my behest, a number of such people living in poverty came to talk at one of the meetings, but rather than telling the committee members what they should do or what policy recommendations should be formulated, they simply described their lives. The impact of their stories became their "gifts" to the committee and was in line with the feelings of many of its members that they had benefitted from these narratives and were beginning to understand what it really means to live in poverty. It was these previously unknown details about their lives that became the basis for many of the recommendations made by that committee.

For the ATD Fourth World Movement and for me, the guiding principle became that families and society were both benefactors and beneficiaries when they were truly in touch with each other. This eventually enabled me to put into words how we, as parents, benefited from what our children contributed to us, as did our so-called "clients" in our "role" as social workers. I also began to understand that it is not so much that democracies were not just not caring enough towards these families, but that by not caring, they were depriving themselves of what the families could contribute to them. Doing so does not refer necessarily to economic activity, but also—unexpectedly—to the tenderness to which we had referred (Rosenfeld and Tardieu, 2000).

This principle also changed my views about what is called "community social work". No longer did I regard its main purpose as assisting the "deprived" populations in our midst with work or income. I am aware that community workers have good reason to represent these populations. This because, as one often discovers that, unexpectedly, people living in poverty have the potential to contribute to their communities. They can contribute "hidden qualities" such as the tenderness from which societies-at-large seem to benefit (Rosenfeld and Tardieu, 2000), and other unknown attributes that families living in poverty apparently possess. What I now realize is that one of the major contributions of families living in poverty to society at large is their ability to make us see "ourselves" as basically all equal, i.e. as being "human" in the full sense of the word. For instance, individuals in authority can—through the narratives of family members —identify with those living in poverty and thus see themselves as somehow similar to them. To restate my point, these are the kinds of benefits that "we", the more privileged in society, can gain from our on reciprocity-based relating to these families.

This paradigmatic, rarely acknowledged, shift was significant for me because it linked work with the poorest in our midst to reciprocity. If reciprocity is the name of the game, then each partner has something from which the other partners can benefit. It is the same kind of reciprocity as that found in the spirit of what Winnicott (1953) wrote: "There is nothing like a mother, only a mother and a child", i.e. the reciprocal mother-child relationship. The challenge that ensued for us from this insight was to accept and to make use of this reciprocity, the contributions of these formerly-excluded as a significant means for overcoming exclusion by society.

## 4. "ARTISANS OF DEMOCRACY": WHAT MIGHT "LEARNING COMPANIONS" DO TO ENABLE ORGANIZATIONS TO CONTRIBUTE TO MOVES BEYOND EXCLUSION

Ever since my initial meetings with them, I have continued to engage with ATD Fourth World Movement as one of their "allies" or partners, in a role which we came to call "learning companions". "Learning companions" engage in "reciprocal learning", which, in this context, is effective when used for on action-based and mutually beneficial transactions. They facilitate unexpected learning when each participant is open to the other. It is the kind of awakening to the "the other" that lies at the heart of what "learning companions" do. The idea is that in the course of reciprocal learning transformative opportunities emerge. "The craft of learning companions" is one that has served members of ATD Fourth World Movement in various countries and is based on "reflective learning", which is learning requiring a minimum of hierarchy.

Some ten years ago I had the good fortune to start working with Bruno Tardieu, a long-time member of the ATD Fourth World Volunteer Corps, on a book called, *Artisans of Democracy—How Ordinary People, Families in Extreme Poverty, and Social Institutions become Allies to Overcome Social Exclusion* (Rosenfeld and Tardieu, 2000). In this publication, instead of describing the craft of engaging directly with families living in extreme poverty, we described how members of ATD Fourth World Movement recruit individuals and organizations to act for the benefit of families living in extreme poverty through a strategy that, to the best of my knowledge, had never been documented before. Our work on this book was inspired and accompanied by my friend and colleague, the late Donald Schön. In preparing this volume, we interviewed representatives of twelve organizations that had made changes in the lives of families living in poverty, including the Electric Company of France (EDF), The Economic and Social Council of France, a journalist in a newspaper of Basel ("Basler Zeitung") and a spokesperson at the United Nations. The goal of these joint-learning meetings was to understand the "actionable knowledge" that had enabled members of ATD Fourth World Movement and others to recruit organizations and engage them in actions on behalf of families living in extreme poverty. Among the many, what we came to call, "Principles of Actions" that were derived from these conversations, we identified one factor which had contributed to furthering the commitment of all twelve interviewees. This was, unexpectedly, the "tenderness" which persons living in poverty revealed about themselves. Realizing this as one common factor in their lives deeply touched members of the organizations, to a large extent because it represented something that, as they reported, was often sorely missing in their own daily work and lives.

An example of this tenderness surfaced, for example, when children from families living in extreme poverty were granted a wish to visit the control room of the Electric Company of France (EDF). During the visit, the children were curious, nice to each other and very grateful for the opportunity that had been granted them. Their behavior created a dissonance for the company officials, since they did not expect them to behave in this manner. And it was this dissonance, in turn, which made their humanity so evident to them. Indeed, the workers were so moved by how the children reacted that eventually the organization ceased its policy of cutting off electricity to such families during the winter months. The formal justification for this change in policy was made when it dawned on members of EDF what had been happening to the second homes of wealthy families that were not used in winter time when the cost of electricity is highest. It turned out that the payments by the wealthy families did not cover the cost of providing them with electricity and had, therefore, to be subsidized. This realization was then used as a justification for subsidizing electricity for people living in poverty who consume electricity the whole year round.

This story is an example of how the kind of committed, creative and powerful "art" used by ATD Fourth World Movement contributes to the well-being of the most excluded people in democracies around the world. The work of twelve such ATD Fourth World Movement sites was showcased in "Artisans of Democracy" (Rosenfeld and Tardieu, 2000), which by now has been translated into five languages. This is an indication that the previously unidentified knowledge of people living in poverty was considered very valuable. It has thus become apparent to us that when presented in actionable terms, the implicit knowledge revealed in "Emergence from Extreme Poverty" and in "Artisans of Democracy", is effective in recruiting societal resources for families living in extreme poverty. For example, the discovery of the unexpected impact of tenderness in the work of ATD Fourth World Movement provides an explicit guideline on how to serve both the un(der)served and their society. However unique this case may be, the heart of the book shows how to recruit societal resources for the benefit of a wide variety of "unseen poor" in different societies. More widely, actions like those presented in "Artisans of Democracy" may well be an important contribution to strengthening and implementing the values of democracy among those who would normally not profit from them.

## 5. FROM LEARNING THAT "ONLY THE BEST IS 'GOOD ENOUGH'" TO INTRODUCING THE 17$^{TH}$ OF OCTOBER – THE WORLD DAY FOR THE ERADICATION OF POVERTY – INTO THE KNESSET (PARLIAMENT) OF ISRAEL

My acquaintance with the ATD Fourth World Movement began in seminars relating to research in poverty in the 1970s (Rosenfeld, 1989) (Rosenfeld and Tardieu, 2000), and most recently enabled my colleagues and me in Israel to introduce the 17$^{th}$ of October—the World Day for the Eradication of Poverty—to the Knesset (Parliament) of Israel, for the first time in 2009.

As I came to learn, "Fourth World" refers to the "fourth estate" consisting of the unseen poor who had no representation in the French Parliament during the French Revolution where only the aristocracy, the bourgeoisie, and the proletariat were among the "états" (estates) represented there.

ATD Fourth World Movement was founded by Father Joseph Wresinski in 1957, in France, and its center is at Méry-sur-Oise to the north of Paris. It now has teams in over thirty countries and members of the Permanent Forum

Against Extreme Poverty in over one hundred countries. Its commitment is to the lives of people living in extreme poverty and exclusion in different countries and who are thought of as "a people". The movement is composed of three groups: first, are the members of the Permanent Volunteer Corps composed of around 450 individuals who are paid minimum wages irrespective of their responsibilities, their years of work and their qualifications, and who mostly work full time; the second group is composed of families living in extreme poverty who have been called "activists"; third, and finally, there are the "allies", a group to which I and many others belong and who contribute to the work of ATD Fourth World Movement according to their interests and its needs.

Since I joined this movement I have been involved in their undertaking—to further the eradication of extreme poverty—and as I know now "if you are with ATD be prepared for a never-ending series of surprises (Peters and Waterman, 1982)".

When I went to visit their headquarters in Méry-sur-Oise and their archives in Baillet-en-France, I met many committed individuals and families such as Louis Join Lambert and his wife Mascha. I also met the late Bernadette Cornuau and the late Francine de la Gorce, a French Jewess, both of whom were among the first to join Père Joseph Wresinski, as well as Eugen Brand, for many years the Head of the International Leadership Team of ATD Fourth World Movement. I mention them not only because of my gratitude to them and our friendship, but also to avoid following their own, excessive self-imposed quest for anonymity when there is so much that I learned with and from them during the decades of our acquaintance.

It took me quite some time to accustom myself to what ATD Fourth World Movement stood for. What I knew from my first visit was what Père Joseph had told me about families living in extreme poverty and exclusion. It included the generative ideas I had learned from him at the beginning of our acquaintance, when he told me that for those living in extreme poverty "only the best is good enough", and that "those living in poverty have something to contribute to the world", and that "the poor are a people". I emphasize these points because a central principle of action is to help those living in poverty to be seen and to see themselves differently than in the past. For instance, doing so as a collective results in moving from beyond where they had been before.

Even as I discovered more and more about the work of the ATD Fourth World Movement, I found that I was still reluctant to see myself as one of its allies and to disseminate their impressive modes of working. My reluctance ended when I discovered that this movement, headed by a Catholic priest, was not a Christian "missionary" enterprise but a humanist one. Indeed, my concern about it being a missionary enterprise was allayed when I dared to share this concern with Bernadette Cornuau, who explained that if it were a missionary movement she would never have joined it. This statement and my fascination with the movement's ways of learning and acting enabled me to become one of its "allies". This occurred during a visit to Bernadette at her home in Herblay, near Paris, where she lived in the midst of many families living in extreme poverty. I was speechless when I saw Bernadette's interaction with her neighbors, a mother and child living in extreme poverty. At a certain point, the child misbehaved—I don't remember exactly what he did. Anyway, when his mother scolded and hit him, I distinctly remember how Bernadette responded. She told the woman, quite firmly, that if she wanted to hit her child, she had to take him outside because she did not allow anyone who was in her home to be hit. That was the end of the mother threatening her child and, for me, a dawning understanding that it would be worthwhile to take time to fathom what ATD Fourth World Movement was all about. What I came to understand was that out of respect for the mother and her child Bernadette did not want to tell her what to do and yet she was very clear about what was acceptable to her and what she was not ready to condone.

One reason why Bernadette's reaction has remained etched in my memory is because I had often wondered what members of ATD Fourth World Movement do when faced with violence in their encounters with families. A violent incident might stop some social workers from engaging in their work with the family. The way Bernadette responded became an example of the unexpected manner in which ATD Fourth World Movement related to these families. There were other examples of my encounters with Bernadette and ATD's unforeseen ways of engaging with families: on Fridays she would take two or three families to go shopping with her; on certain days they met to sing songs by Johannes Brahms with the families. When I expressed my astonishment that they sang these songs and not songs with which the families were familiar, she reminded me that, "they sang these songs because," quoting the famous words of Père Joseph, "only the best is good enough for them." This confirmed my belief that there was much to learn about the ways of ATD Fourth World Movement.

Another unforgettable surprise came in 1987, when I was invited to the first World Day for the Eradication of Extreme Poverty, before it had been declared an official United Nations day. The day comprised a ceremony that took place on the Trocadéro Plaza in the heart of Paris, which had recently been renamed the "Square of Human Rights and Freedoms". It took time for me to fully understand the meaning of that event and how crucial it was for raising world-wide concern for families living in extreme poverty, those who were neither seen nor heard. I needed time to understand how important this annual event, in more and more countries, was for raising concern about them and their lives.

What struck me more than anything else on that occasion were two events: the *first* was that ATD Fourth World Movement had invited many families living in extreme poverty from other countries to take part in the events of the "Day". Over 100,000 people, both privileged and under-privileged were there. What was even more amazing was that these families from France and from other countries were hosted by local families from different walks of life who, as I was told, were allies of ATD who lived in Paris.

The *other* unforgettable facet of this event was the different kinds of stands which had been prepared especially for the event. They included computers, books, songs, story-telling, arts and crafts activities, and games. While some of these stands were intended to introduce children to new things, others were there to inform visitors about the lives of children from different countries living in extreme poverty.

These stands provided information about "Tapori", an Indian expression referring to children who begged and then shared money in the streets of Bombay. Tapori has become a worldwide movement of children, including those living in extreme poverty in many different countries.

In each of these stands, members of ATD Fourth World Movement and of other organizations introduced themselves to families and children living in poverty and exclusion from different countries. I shall always remember how someone said, "Here, in the middle of Paris, in the Gardens of the Trocadero, you families and children living in extreme poverty are our invited guests."[4] These words of Pere Joseph, engraved in the marble which, translated into English, mean: "Wherever men and women are condemned to live in extreme poverty, human rights are violated. To come together to ensure that these rights be respected is our solemn duty".

The importance of that event became clearer to me when, in 1992, the United Nations declared the 17th of October as the "World Day for the Eradication of Extreme Poverty" and called for its introduction into the parliament of each country.

In the wake of all this, several colleagues as well as people living in extreme poverty came together in 2009 to initiate the introduction of the World Day for the Eradication of Extreme Poverty in the Knesset (Israel's parliament). This event was a milestone for us and we are gradually "discovering" that extreme poverty also exists in Israel, and that we could and should take every opportunity to work towards its eradication. The 17th of October has become an established reminder for the unseen poor in Israel to be seen and heard. I believe that by introducing this event in the Knesset, which has taken place five times, the awareness of their existence has been raised significantly. Initially, there were only four Members of the Knesset who agreed to sponsor the event, there are now more than nineteen sponsoring organizations.

Needless to say, much work is still needed to make it a more meaningful day, not just for talking about poverty but for introducing legislation and concern for the poorest in our midst. This is of special relevance for the most religious communities as well as for the immigrants from Ethiopia and especially for the Arab population. Recently, the core group engaged in introducing this event to the Knesset is in the process of establishing, together with other Knesset members, a permanent Forum for the Eradication of Extreme Poverty and Exclusion in Israel. There is a long journey ahead and this annual event might be one of its beginnings.

Related to these special days in the Knesset, it may be well to mention that the first Israel National Committee for the Eradication of Poverty, of which I was a member, was established in 2013.

## 6. LEARNING FOR ACTION IN AN INTERNATIONAL SEMINAR SPONSORED BY THE ATD FOURTH WORLD MOVEMENT[5]

Over recent decades, the International ATD Fourth World Movement has worked on many fronts to explore the theme of "Unleashing Hidden Potential" as a means for unearthing knowledge and capacities that people living in poverty have rarely had the opportunity to share (Defraigne-Tardieu, 2002). This situation arises either because families living in extreme poverty themselves do not recognize their own potential or when people living in close proximity fail to do so. In early 1995, ATD Fourth World Movement in the United States initiated work around this theme at the time that Genevieve Defraigne-Tardieu and Bruno Tardieu had moved to Boston. They looked for academics in the field of education who were concerned with equal opportunities for children, built strong relationships with academics from the Harvard School of Education, Tufts, Boston University, and the Massachusetts Institute of Technology and involved them in very fruitful reflections.

### Warwick-New York—A Learning Seminar on Unleashing Hidden Potential

After prolonged preparations, in 2000 I attended a seminar on this topic held in Warwick, New York. Its explicit goal was to "bring together parents, classroom teachers, community workers, university professors of education and sociology and full-time members of the Permanent Volunteer Corps of the ATD Fourth World Movement." Fifty people attended and each of the participants contributed a story documenting an experience in which he/she witnessed some surprising "hidden potential" that a child had "unleashed", and I was one of them.

I contributed the story of Samy that illustrates the kinds of "exclusion" I had come to know.

> It was a story from the beginning of my career when a twelve year old fatherless child, who lived away from his mother in a kibbutz in Israel, was

about to be expelled from the kibbutz because he had stolen money to purchase materials for building a radio transmitter. On one of my monthly visits to consult the counselor, I advised him to take the boy aside and ask him to explain what had happened. The counselor first talked to the mother and then to the boy. The mother shared with the counselor some family history that Samy himself had never been told. During the Holocaust the boy had survived for several years alone without his parents, while hidden by a family that ultimately saved his life. Soon after his parents returned, Samy and his mother went to Palestine, while the father, an engineer, stayed behind "to provide maintenance on radio transmitters used to save Jewish survivors on their way out to Palestine". In the meantime the father died but the mother had never told her son that his father had died. In stealing the money for buying parts for the radio transmitter, Samy had planned to reach his father whom he believed was still alive.

This was the first time that anyone had heard or spoken about Samy's family and was the first time Samy learned that his father would not return. Such silence and denial was common after the Holocaust and was often the practice in the newly-founded State of Israel.

This incident had consequences, some of which I only heard about several years later: first, Samy was not expelled from the kibbutz; second, he was given resources and help to build a radio transmitter and eventually Samy became an engineer; third, Samy's counselors and peers were transformed by this experience. This story paved the way for those in charge and the others in his group to overcome their reluctance to talk, grieve, and accompany Samy and others with whom they talked about their hidden pasts and suffering. This freed them to engage in their new society, to join and, eventually, to contribute to it.

The goal of the seminar was to enable people from different disciplines to learn together. It included participants from various professions and walks of life: academics; teachers; parents of children who were underachievers and whose schools did not tap into the learning abilities of those living in extreme poverty (in contrast to what they did with other children). The parents present were involved with the ATD Fourth World Movement and their children benefited from the innovative street libraries program in their neighborhoods.

I found the idea of "unleashing", which means "to release or to free from restraints or controls"[6] both moving and impressive. To begin with, I felt uneasy because the seminar struggled to discover a common mind-set for its heterogeneous participants, until I realized that it takes a movement rather than "the groves of academe" to engage in a learning event with such a wide range of participants. As it happened, it did allow each of the participants to find his/her voice, which enabled a kind of unforeseen discourse to emerge. In hindsight, what impressed me in this encounter was that uncovering and acknowledging what one does not know is a powerful source of knowledge, likely to contribute to the individual and the collective. For someone interested in both learning from success and actionable knowledge, the work of the seminar was fascinating. It showed clearly how the extraction of hidden knowledge contributes to practice and towards the achievement of desired goals.. It also revealed that that way of working is a craft and one that ATD Fourth World Movement continues to practice and share with the world through its ongoing work. That this tool can be used, will be described below, in a variety of ways in different stages of transformative work, in diverse settings, and by a variety of partners when all of them are open to striving for the reversal of social and economic exclusion.

While the seminar sought to minimize "the false and painful division between people seen as experts and people seen as recipients of help and advice", I am reminded now, over ten years later, of how unexpected the process was and how relevant and compelling the ideas still remain.

Looking back, I recall that one of the most important elements in the success of the seminar was how much thought, care and love was invested in its planning. It enabled every single participant to have an active role and to expect sharing what emerged. It was understood that every one of us had something to contribute rather than remain passive. Accordingly, each invitee wrote a story related to the seminar topic so that each person was by definition and from the start a contributor. As I now know, this is the kind of process that encourages the revealing of "hidden potential" and the uncovering of vulnerability, both of which can lead to advancing reciprocity. It was this process which turned the seminar into a "joint venture".

Telling stories requires experience, trust and hard work. That is why it was so important for all participants to prepare their "seed stories" for their own "group of participants" ahead of time. For the parents it was very important to write a seed story so they could become aware of their knowledge—their unknown knowledge. Telling stories was important for building an eagerness to learn from others, something that started even before the people got together at the seminar, because in thinking about what story to present, participants were made aware of what they could give to and share with others. This was a perfect example of how to enhance "creative reciprocity".

A good example of this point was that the telling of stories enabled a university professor in charge of a teachers' training program to meet a woman who was living in a shelter and raising a large family by herself. The professor was amazed at the conversation they had and was deeply moved by this encounter which became a highlight in her understanding of the children's situation in school.

What interested me most was anything connected to overcoming the intolerable school failure of children who had come from a poor background. Some progress was made possible by those who believed that parents raising their children in poverty have specific knowledge about their children and about what was good for them. This was based on the belief that parents, knowingly or unknowingly, owned that "actionable knowledge", which is rarely considered to be of benefit to other children, including those who do not live in poverty. That seminar participants thought about these things, was one expression of the belief that well-prepared people from different walks of life *can* think together.

Because of these preparations and because people were not introduced to each other according to their social status, participants felt themselves to be equal stakeholders and partners. As such, the entire seminar was a joint venture, aimed at showing how to overcome the unacceptably high rate of failure of children in school that was attributed to their having come from a poor background. To move beyond this situation not only required relying on the experience, trust and hard work of many individuals, but it also necessitated a concrete process of creating reciprocity in which the action related knowledge of parents raising their children in poverty—which had rarely been sought out in other contexts—could be easily accepted. That this knowledge could be useful for many children, including those who do not live in poverty, was supported by the belief that people from different walks of life can think together and that to do so needed this kind of caring-in-advance preparations.

I had never participated in an event where flowers, a poem on peace or origami cranes (symbols of peace) made by the children of the New York street libraries were placed on participants' pillows as tokens of their support for the success of the seminar. Such tiny gestures are fine examples of what Père Joseph meant when he said that, "The poor deserve the best . . . ." This image, of a simple bed made up as if in the most luxurious hotel on the face of the earth, really describes the atmosphere of the event. Only the highest quality was considered "good enough" for guests, and immediately upon arrival one sensed the respect, seriousness, commitment, and caring with which the organizers attended to their guests from different walks of life.

Four different categories of people attended the seminar: trainers; parents; community workers; and academics. All were deeply invested in the proceedings. Until now I remain amazed at how the organizers chose participants from such very different walks of life but made sure that their social statuses were not introduced, so that every single person was recognized as both an equal stakeholder and a partner. To provide a variety of perspectives on children's education, four stories were chosen for joint discussions. The stories were written by a parent, a teacher, a street library worker, and a young father looking back at his childhood when he too had benefited from street libraries. In this setting discussions could not be abstract. Each person would present her/his own story so that others could become aware of their own unknown knowledge. Then the group together with each story-teller responded and discussed what had been shared. The groups were mixed and this was also a real challenge for me. When I tried to find what was a common denominator to their actions, I found that many of the participants were strangers to me, and I to them, on many levels, not just because I had never met them before, but also because I rarely come into such close contact with people living in extreme poverty. Compared to a conversation I could have with one of my peer groups, the discourse in this mixed group was very different because it was fraught with dissonance, from which I learned a great deal. This setting created an unusual eagerness to learn from each other as each participant was seen as a potential source of knowledge. Since this was so persistently emphasized, it contributed to the introduction of "reciprocal learning".

One technique used in the seminar was particularly useful for eliciting findings. In order to uncover shared experiences of the four different mixed groups, similar questions were discussed: What was "progress" or "success"? What was achieved? What obstacles were overcome? What had contributed to the progress? What structures or tools had helped?

Our principal finding related to what children saw as the factors facilitating their learning. For instance, one unexpected finding was that the children who learned best were those who were proud of their parents. It became evident that this pride, in turn, encouraged the schools to treat the parents with greater respect. Similarly, when the parents and teachers saw themselves as partners, as both beneficiaries and benefactors, all in the triangle—child, parent, teacher—they were able to benefit from differences in the observations presented. Applying these findings to the parents, I concluded that when parents were proud of themselves their self-esteem and capacities inevitably soared. That the relationships between parents and teachers could be reciprocal was a kind of revelation for me as I had never considered this kind of reciprocity before.

Another innovative tactic employed at this seminar was to have the Steering Committee composed of representatives of all the different groups of people which enabled each of these diverse individuals to dare to speak out and share with the others what he/she thought.

Importantly, discussions never crystallized around theories. Rather, we were all encouraged to focus on actions. As I had learned from Donald Schön, the best way to obtain knowledge that is relevant for action is by avoiding explanations and emphasizing descriptions of what had worked in the past and what one can currently know. When this happens, participants and partners can act on the assumption that their actions will also be effective in and for the future.

What was initially so surprising and disturbing, is that in the beginning it was so hard for academics to listen without being patronizing. They were genuinely surprised that women living in poverty were able to contribute to the conversation in very significant ways, and that ATD Fourth World Movement leaders encouraged them to do so. In time it became obvious to the academics that people living in poverty do have much to contribute to the conversation.

To illustrate, I shall mention an excerpt from the story of one of the participants in the seminar.

## The Story of Nixon Pacheco—A Young Father

Nixon Pacheco, a young man who had grown up in poverty and who was now a young father, was *not* asked *why* he did this or that, but only asked *what* he did. Hence, in our discussions what was created was an ambiance based on exchanges related to real experiences. This illustrated, at least for me, that one is more inclined to listen in a group if people are speaking about their real lives.

> You have to learn who you are before you can learn who everybody else is. That is what Fourth World did for me. Fanchette and Vincent and all the members of the Permanent Volunteer Corps always showed a lot of respect for my family, for my grandfather. They helped me get a sense of history, of the big picture. They helped me see who my grandfather really was. He was a symbol. To me he was like Moses. He led us into the unknown, to give us a better chance. Coming from Puerto Rico, he came into the unknown, and not knowing what to expect gave us a chance at making it. He probably saw the big picture. Coming from Puerto Rico to the US meant taking a chance. Moses never saw the Promised Land and my grandpa never saw his family getting out of poverty. Martin Luther King never saw interracial couples walking down the street like we do now as an everyday event. But I dreamt about how my grandfather never saw me graduating from high school, even though he was the one who showed me how important it would be for him and the family, if I did so. This is why I have these values today and that I believe that I am able to pass it on to my daughter.

These words made me think about the relationship between learning from success and learning from "surprise". When people are free enough to want to know something, it forces them to review what they are already thinking without making it explicit. People who are always trying to confirm what they know are never exposed to reviewing what they had been thinking. As John Maynard Keynes (Keynes, 1936) said, "the difficulty lies not so much in developing new ideas as in escaping from old ones". The meaning of this became clearer to me during the seminar. Perhaps when one is focused on success, one is already ready to be surprised, and that is why surprise itself is such a crucial part of learning. So if you look at success or at what has succeeded, you inevitably open the minds of people. This may then free them from their preconceived ideas and take them away from discussions *about* children rather than *with* them. The surprise about what creates success is that it leads to eagerness to explore and to learn what works for children.

There are many reasons for learning from success rather than from failure and a prime one is that it taps into lessons from situations in which there is little codified knowledge. Another is that, after a time, being able to succeed no longer needs to be seen as a surprise. Indeed, being in the throes of uncertainty, as when you gamble and fail, often raises an inevitable quest for surprise.

## 7. REFLECTIVE ONGOING LEARNING FROM SUCCESS: A CHANCE FOR A MOVEMENT AND OTHERS WITH A MISSION OF CHANGE

There can be little doubt that systematic "Learning from Success" is not very common. In contrast, learning from failure is used persistently by many organizations, such as the army. I have found that whenever I introduce the idea of learning from success, the almost automatic response is most often "Why not learn from failure?" The question, then, is whether learning from success is more effective than learning from failure. Whereas some see learning from success as an outlandish gimmick, others see the refusal to use it and the insistence on learning from failure as a way to retain failure as an excuse. Be that as it may, learning from success, requires one to be ready to engage in retrospective learning; that is to put into the language of actions that worked in the past as actions that can be used for the present and the future.

However, as I have been explaining, we should go ahead and use learning from success in order to discover ways of action that have been effective in the past, as a means—for instance—for learning how to fight poverty. This can be justified by claiming, as the founder of ATD Fourth World Movement said, "Poverty is manmade and man can unmake it". But there is another dimension here, an emotional or motivational one, like getting in touch with something that was not there before their having experienced that success. When this is the case, when success emanates from the unknown and uncontrollable, it has neither an author nor a sage who deserves to be hailed and venerated. As such, no one has a claim to the result of success, except perhaps those who have acquired the expertise to know how to bring it about by learning from success.

The idea of developing a mode of learning based on successes in the past for the future emerged from this seminar. We found that this collective action, within which each stakeholder becomes a learner identifying what has led to success, involves elements of personal creation or invention. Such actions occur with a minimum of hierarchy and are a product of collegiate learning. A world which is continuously inventing interventions requires settings that are geared towards both ongoing and collective learning.

In light of this, employing "learning from success" as a preferred mode of learning provides opportunities for addressing unresolved issues, because such openings are more likely to emerge from collective learning rather than from the wisdom of any individual. They also provide opportunities for people used to failing and to being considered failures, to discover their capacity to be learners. They can achieve this by engaging in the generation of generosity that accompanies such learning in settings with which they are not familiar. This point is especially relevant for settings which have been dominated by mind-sets and traditions of very different modes of learning and not so much by learning for action. To reiterate, learning here means gaining-knowledge-for-action and not for developing theories or focusing on explanations.

This point does not mean that the crafts emanating from learning from success cannot be used as a basis for later developing common principles of actions and discovering theories sorely missing in the pursuit of serving the excluded in our midst. It also does not mean that learning from success is a totally new invention which can be of use in pursuits which are change-oriented. One thing we have discovered, though, is that both learning from success and readiness to engage in long-term learning which addresses the needs of the most excluded and come about where there is readiness, generosity and a sense of humor. Whenever these are available, learning from success is more than likely.

In light of this, while it may be easy to introduce learning from success to the least well-provided in human services, it is more difficult to do so without ongoing learning. This is true even though ongoing learning is most essential where there is complexity, ongoing change and a dearth of on achievements-based knowledge. It is in these fields that the capacities and structures of ongoing learning are most essential and called for, since they are the fields where tacit "actionable knowledge" of the past is most likely to be a source of knowledge for the future. It is with this in mind that the Unit of Learning from Success has gained experience and developed the three Methods of Learning from Success (see Appendices II and III) which also provide a guide for introducing ongoing learning.

## NOTES

*ATD—Initially Aide a toute Detresse ("All Together in Distress"), later "Agir tous pour la Dignite" (All Together for Dignity).

1. Joshua 6:1.

2. At this point "learning companions" are being formally trained at the "Workshop for Learning Companions", which is a series of 4-5 hour, semi-monthly sessions over half a year at the Myers Brookdale JDC Institute. At the end of the workshop, each of the participants is asked to present a case describing his/her work in a setting of his/her choice in which learning

from success has been introduced. After these workshops attempts are made to find opportunities for continued contact with the accruing number of past participants.

3. Cycle d'Etude Europeen "Les familles socialement défavorisées", Bienne, Switzerland, organized by the European Section of the United Nations, August 16-25, 1970.

4. This statement is reminiscent of what was written on the monument of Napoleon, in the Place d'Invalides: "I wish my ashes to rest on the banks of the Seine among the people of France whom I so much loved ".

5. I would like to express my thanks to Dr. Genevieve Defraigne-Tardieu for helping me in writing this Part.

6. Collins English Dictionary—Harper-Collins, 1979.

# VIII

# Epilogue: "Genocide" and "Poverty" — Two Collective Man-Made Evils of Our Epochs: A Challenge for the Future*

> A man lives not only his personal life as an individual,
> but also, consciously or unconsciously,
> the life of his epoch and his contemporaries.
> Thomas Mann (1924)

Here I am, at the end of writing a book with three major themes:

1. The move from exclusion to reciprocity as the mission of the social work profession and beyond it.
2. "Learning from success" as a source for knowing how to act in complex situations.
3. To share with people not just interested in "explaining the world" but in "changing it". Among them, the initiators of the book—The ATD Fourth World Movement.

Thus, a major point of the book is to see "exclusion" (also "being un(der)served") as a state of being with minimum opportunities to be of benefit to others and to benefit from them, i.e. of reciprocity. To achieve this requires settings equipped for engaging in ongoing learning by initiating and then introducing reciprocity, which lend themselves to reciprocally beneficial exchanges. In turn, this refers to exchanges committed to bringing about change in complex situations by reconstructing what had worked in such situations in the past and may do so again in the present and for the future. "Learning from success", i.e. from actions that had had a desired impact in complex situations in the past, can serve as a leverage for learning how to employ them in the present and for the benefit of the future.

In line with this, I decided to end the book with the following challenge for the future: To consider how to deliberately and daringly address two collective, man-made evils that have so far never been persistently and effectively addressed, and this with a view of eradicating them, i.e. to do more than standing by their victims, counting them and learning their histories. I refer to genocide and extreme poverty. Addressing these two phenomena means that rather than proposing theories and explanations, it requires finding ways of dealing with each on the basis of distinctive, effective action-oriented knowledge of the past. Doing so, especially vis-à-vis genocide, is bound to seem quite foreign and unlikely to succeed because of the utter helplessness of the world and its leaders in the face of these so extremely persistent, belligerent and bellicose world-wide realities. While poverty is also man-made, it is different from genocide. It is not that same initial, quite varied ideas relating to both phenomena have not been voiced, but neither of them has evoked deliberate actions or investments in eradicating them either. With regard to genocide, Hannah Arendt (1963), herself seriously threatened by the Holocaust, challenged conventional views of it. She claimed that there was an ongoing "lack of thinking" related to the Holocaust and to both the helplessness and submissiveness of the Jews as well as of the non-Jewish leadership. Perhaps, since her argument was formulated as an attack and not as a challenge, it has provided little ground for discourse on what to *do* concerning genocide. Her views contrast with what is reflected in the correspondence between Einstein and Freud (1932), where the idea of "Why War?" was raised. While their discussion on preventing war centered on "thinking" *about* genocide, their exchanges led to explaining this evil, rather than to initiating actions related to its eradication. They did not consider, for instance, effective "learning from success", i.e. actions which in the past had been effective for counteracting genocides, as an alternative to what is happening in the present and thus also for the future. This is based on my contention that reflecting on what had been done somewhere, at some time in the past, and had had even *some* impact in counteracting genocide as the man-made evil it is, might be a start to initiating thinking about how not to remain bystanders of genocide, let alone how not to become its victims.

After raising this issue at the end of this volume I decided to concretize it by relating my experience in psychotherapy with one victim of the Holocaust. It is an example of how to act in the aftermath of this genocide, even though it only addresses the impact of the "fear of weakness" in contrast to "the fear of freedom" (Fromm, 1942). It reflects work with a middle-aged man born in Germany and who lived there with his father who was a pastor and his mother, an unfeeling woman. Both his parents had voted for the Nazi Party and when he was a boy he had been beaten and abused. For instance, his father had once beaten him cruelly when he had come home late after acquiring a bird cage. Later, he read an account of this incident in his father's diary. There is where he wrote that after his son's coming home late one could have heard a "concert", i.e. his son's crying after being beaten for returning late. As if that were not enough, when he was five years old, his mother sent him to his grandmother and then disappeared for half a year.

As an adult, he married an unfeeling woman and, after the birth of several children, they divorced. In the years that followed he tried to improve his relationship with his children and, after several years of psychoanalysis, he married a kind, caring woman. Later, during psychotherapy with me, he gradually got in touch with how he had been completely unseen in his parental home and how he could not have allowed himself to open this issue with his German therapists. In time, it dawned on him that his parents had been enemies of his weakness, as of any weakness, including their own. He realized that he had never dared to face and understand that his parents' abhorrence of human weakness—their own, his as well as anyone else's—had forced him to become a victim of evil. It was his helplessness in the face of the cruelty of his parents, and their tolerance vis-à-vis the extermination of Jews, that may well have been related to their counteracting any weakness they saw in themselves - the weakness against which they were expected and instructed to harden themselves ("abhaerten" in German) and which was one of the hallmarks of their German upbringing. Thus, his own and many others' acceptance of annihilating the "weak" Jews was a "means" to eradicate any of their own and their children's weaknesses. Because of this, in hindsight, he had unconsciously chosen me, a Jewish therapist, and this may well be what had made it possible to address a theme, which in his previous two psychoanalyses and one additional experience of psychotherapy, he had never been able to address and understand.

In this connection, I dare mention the *one* element which may well be at the root of each of the two man-made evils addressed here—genocide and extreme poverty—as in other situations in which people cannot face their own individual and collective weakness. I believe that the inability of the Germans to face their own individual and any collective's weakness was at the root of the genocide named the "Holocaust", as a man-made collective evil. It is related to each of the Nazis' gigantic and devastating fear of both their own individual and any collective's weakness. It is that that had made them resort to introducing and inventing their own collective commitment to destroying the Jews who were, for them, the epitome—if not the symbol—of any personal and collective helplessness and weakness. They're not experiencing and confronting the consequences of what they attributed to Jews as a collective and as individuals, may well be at the root of their collective acts of evil. The latter because they were not able to accept and come to terms with their own weakness and helplessness. By considering the Jews as a collective of outsiders who did not belong, made it possible to inflict the Holocaust on them. Indeed man-made transparency, like when the victims of genocide tend not to be seen, may well be at its root, and thus a key for how to act in the future—i.e., to ensure transparency. This, as such, may well be a key to move beyond it.

Now with regard to the eradication of poverty, that it is not addressed is most clear with regard to the poorest of the poor in our midst, who are those who are not seen by dominant collectives as individuals and, as such, as not belonging to them. Indeed, what is similar to both is that both are man-made, nay collectively man-made and, if so, as Pere Joseph, the founder of the Fourth World Movement, said, "poverty is man-made and man can unmake it". But then, to achieve this requires a global determination to establish two separate world-wide undertakings directed at the eradication of each of these evils—genocide and poverty—equipped with a readiness "to think", which as Hannah Arendt claimed the Jewish leaders during the Holocaust and any others were not able to do.

With regard to poverty, and based on "learning from success", we should appreciate the achievements of the ATD Fourth World Movement vis-a-vis the poorest of the poor living in extreme poverty and exclusion which I have had the privilege to witness over the past four decades. I have learned about some of their effective, actionable knowledge related to "fighting poverty", which is supported in the recent publication of their long-term study—"Extreme Poverty is Violence" (Defraigne-Tardieu, 2012).

So what is to be done?

I hope that these two "evils of our epoch" will be seen as an invitation to consider how to address both of them as "global callings". Consequently, I end this book with a call to address each of these two man-made evils separately, and a call to those affected by each of them not to remain helpless bystanders. This means to start out by accepting and then addressing the roots of each of these two universal collective man-made evils—genocide and poverty—separately, and each on a world-wide basis. Doing so separately is imperative, in order to be able to get at the roots of what is unique to each of these "evils"—a distinct commitment to first address what is related to each of them, and then to move towards learning together and from each other how to address the likes of them.

To suggest engaging in each, let alone in both, determinedly and on a world-wide basis, might be considered pretentious if not overstated. Yet I believe that to do so *does* open ways for putting both of them on the global agenda for the good of the future.

While I close my writing with the need to address each of them separately, *how* to do so goes beyond the scope of this book. However, this does not go beyond my conviction that it *is* a matter of first thinking and then as acting, i.e. it becoming and being in "our" hands. This enables me to end by quoting what my friend and colleague, Genevieve Defraigne-Tardieu of ATD Fourth World Movement, wrote about extreme poverty to me upon reading parts of this book:

> It is all about helping people to escape the fatality of their suffering . . . to free them(selves) from the evil of the Holocaust or from any "evil" which, on whatever grounds, had deprived them of their dignity.

As a member of the profession of social work, I shall end by emphasizing that social work, as a profession, should not be afraid of tackling these and other man-made evils that our world faces now, as in the past. None of this is deriding the worth of psychotherapy or for simply expanding the role of community social work and of much that is also valuable. What I am arguing for is that facing genocide and extreme poverty may actually represent a distinct breakthrough for social work. To do so, we need to put back the "social", in its widest and most significant sense, into social work, as one of its missions as a human service profession.

So let challenges and missions to address these two societal evils, which have always concerned me, and in which I have been involved throughout my life, end this book as a challenge for the future for each of them and beyond it (Rosenfeld, 1993; Rosenfeld, 1999; Rosenfeld, 2000).

*With thanks to Dr. Josef Fisher for contributing to the not simple writing of this "epilogue".

# Acknowledgments

For me to write acknowledgements for writing this book and beyond, is not a duty but an opportunity to express my gratitude, and to mention those who are with us and those who are no more. Many of them remain anonymous even though they made such a difference to the lives of countless others and not only to me and my life.

First, my parents, Julius and Johanna Rosenfeld, née Ettlinger, whose humanity, integrity and courage not only were there for me but also saved and supported so many other people who could so easily have become victims of the Nazi persecutions—and because of whom almost all the members of our family were saved. Thanks to my having been a member of this family, I was not only able to "be" but also to "become".

Then, my late mentor and colleague, Pauline Miller-Shereshefsky, who taught me not to remain distant and neutral with persons who needed me but to accompany them in order to bear with them the travesties of abandonment and aloneness. This endeavor was furthered by my late colleagues Shlomit Hoek and Professor Yisrael Katz, later the head of the School of Social Work and the Minister of Welfare. With Shlomit I had my initiation into the practice of child mental health and with Yisrael into person-centered social policy.

At this point I wish to mention members of the ATD Fourth World Movement, who were particularly close to me. I will start with those who are not with us any more: First, Père Joseph Wresinski, the Founder of the Movement; then Baronesse Alwine de Vos van Steenwijk; and finally, Bernadette Cornuau, one of the first members of the Movement who accompanied me during the four decades of our joint pursuits. Then there are those who are with us. Let me start with Eugen and Anne Claire Brand, the former had been for a long time the Head of the International Leadership Team of the Movement. Then there is Louis Join-Lambert, who was the first of the Movement, who I had met, and his so socio-politically-oriented wife Mascha, and then their son Luc, who had spent one year working at a village for Youth in Israel. Next I shall mention Bruno Tardieu, with whom I wrote amongst others "Artisans of Democracy", as well as his wife Genevieve Defragne-Tardieu, and their three special offsprings. To end I would like to mention Jean-Michel Defromont, my co-author of this book, and Michelle his wife, this without spelling out here the nature of my very special partnership and friendship with each of them.

I now come to express my thanks to Jenny Cohen, and Baruch Hochman, and my wife Ruti, who have commented on previous versions of this book and thus improved this one, and Colette Jay who has so caringly edited an earlier and then final version, as well as by Lindsay Talmud and Professor Eyal Ben-Ary, as well as my friend and colleague Ury Kroch.

Finally, there are those who were around and with me. First my colleagues at the Paul Baerwald School of Social Work and Social Policy at the Hebrew University of Jerusalem whose names appear in the book. And then those at the Myers-JDC-Brookdale Institute, first and foremost its head—Professor Jack Habib—and to Beth Zisman, who have been my personal and professional partners, to whom I am grateful for the over twenty-year-long joint commitment and for the help in paving my way, and my friend and colleague Ury Kroch.

Last and never least, Ruti, who, because of my having had the good sense to wait to marry until I was 49, I thank her for the more than forty years of a life of love, partnership and affection. As for our daughters Noa and Yael for whose generosity and reciprocity I am more than grateful.

# Appendix I
# ATD ("All Together in Dignity") — The Fourth World Movement*

In the tradition of movements of humanity toward social justice for all, the ATD (All Together in Dignity) Fourth World Movement seeks to eradicate extreme poverty while promoting the building of peace and understanding between people. Its founder, the late Fr. Joseph Wresinski (1917-1988), said, "By making the most disadvantaged the starting point of our thoughts and the driving force of our action; we are building a community in which life is good to all." ATD Fourth World Movement does not work on behalf of people living in poverty, nor alongside them; in fact, it was founded with and by people living in extreme poverty and exclusion. Père Joseph Wresinski was born into extreme poverty and founded it together with the most disadvantaged among families in Noisy-le-Grand, France, in 1957. ATD Fourth World Movement's members today come from many different countries and backgrounds.

The movement's approach is to seek out people who are often the most isolated or stigmatized. With members of ATD's permanent volunteers living among them in persistent poverty, they are continually learning how to reform their work together with other partners from a wide diversity of social and cultural backgrounds and of beliefs and convictions. The term "Fourth World" is one that people living in extreme poverty and those in solidarity with them in every part of the world use and can use to describe themselves with pride, and is also a term recalling the importance of every person being able to have a political voice in society. ATD Fourth World Movement today has teams and active members in 32 countries around the world. Women and men, young people and children, in villages and low-income neighborhoods who have dared to pool their courage, their minds, their solidarity and their creativity, sometimes at the risk of their lives. All of them have shaped ATD Fourth World Movement as a movement gathering people from all backgrounds in order to think, act and live together differently in order to show how people who have been discriminated against because of poverty, have experiences and thoughts that can lower the barriers separating members from the human family and bar them from contributing to our world.

*Taken from ATD Fourth World. See www.atd-fourthworld.org, or www.unheard-voices.org.

# Appendix II
# The Unit for Learning from Success and Ongoing Learning in Human Services, Myers-JDC-Brookdale Institute

### 1. THE UNIT

The Unit for Learning from Success and Collaborative Ongoing Learning in Human Services was established in 1995 at the Myers-JDC-Brookdale Institute (Appendix I). The Unit was founded by Prof. Jona Rosenfeld. It focuses on the process of learning from success as a catalyst and facilitator for furthering ongoing organizational learning in human service organizations. Its purpose is to encourage individuals to be learners, to encourage groups of individuals to learn together, to assist organizational structures to facilitate ongoing learning in groups, as a tool for ongoing improvement of the ability to achieve their common goals. A guiding principle in this process is that the staff in human service organizations have tacit knowledge that can be turned into "actionable knowledge", which can then be used by all.

The Unit for Learning from Success works with a broad range of human service organizations. Since its establishment, it has developed strong ties and partnerships with the Ministries of Education, Social Affairs and Health, and with other government and voluntary social organizations in Israel and abroad. The unit is part of the international Association for Organizational Learning.

## 2. THE APPROACH TO LEARNING— "LEARNING FROM SUCCESS"

The emphasis on learning from success is based on a number of principles. The following are its guidelines:

1. Learning From Success is an important and powerful tool for overcoming obstacles to learning at both the individual and the group level, and, as such, for ongoing learning. This, with two objectives in mind:

   a. Its inherent optimistic focus introduces a sense of optimism. Some of the participants have at the outset difficulty in thinking, and acknowledging, that they have had any successes until they are helped to recognize them. This realization often becomes a transformative turning point.
   b. It leads to the identification of actions that can impact on the ability of the participants to pursue their mission in more effective ways and this reinforces their further interest in learning.

2. The essence of learning from success and of how to create, manage and enhance the motivation and the capacity of people to learn, is by introducing a structured process of reflecting in and on their previous actions (Schon, 1982, 1983). This is something that individuals very often do not take the time to do. This is made even more acceptable by occurring in a peer group setting where everyone is both contributing and receiving. This here on reciprocity-based learning helps each of the members of the group not just to learn for and from each other, but it enables each to understand and learn from the experience of each and to discover additional perspectives and points of view. Each person becomes both a learner and a sharer of knowledge, and thus both a benefactor and a beneficiary. This enables each person to benefit from the beginning from collective knowledge.

3. To generate these processes, it trains and deploy *external "learning companions"* who help to establish structured learning processes and frameworks, and to also introduce a wide variety of staff to promote effective learning processes.

4. What is needed to institutionalize learning is to establish structured learning frameworks by introducing the Three Methods of Learning:

   a. The First Method—"Retrospective Learning from Success": A structured method for identifying, explicating, and documenting the tacit knowledge underlying past successes.
   b. The Second Method— "Prospective Learning": Each organization is asked to identify its own "prospective learning questions" for the future, i.e. which address either crucial and unresolved present quests or

issues which are at the heart of its mission. These questions are formulated as learning questions or learning quests.

c. The Third Method— "Learning about Learning": Once organizations have reflected upon and identified their modes and styles of learning, they are able to engage in discourse and to deploy the actionable knowledge that had been gained and thus develop the capacity to engage in seeking and identifying their own modes of both ongoing and effective learning.

5. Finally, an important part of strategy is to create a movement of groups that mutually reinforce the capacity of each to identify and to develop its own modes and networks of learning. This occurs when they come together to share and reinforce their efforts in regional and national events where they can identify both common and different modes of learning, and to identify and choose those that serve them best.

6. The program is intended for individuals and organizations to engage in an ongoing search for opportunities for peer learning, for modes of learning which are most suitable to them so as to further both their individual and collective vision.

These ideas have been developed over the years together with, Israel Sykes and Tsila Weiss, the latter of the Ministry of Education, and more recently Irit Aizik, Ruti Biran, Sarit Ellenbogen-Frankovits, and Orna Shemer, to whom I am more than grateful for their generous commitment and shared learning quest.

Since 2006, Sarit Ellenbogen-Frankovitz served as the deputy director of the unit and she became its director in 2013, and since then the unit is continuing to develop, flourish and publish its work.

# Appendix III
# The Three Methods of Learning from Success

*THE FIRST METHOD:* THE RETROSPECTIVE METHOD – LEARNING FROM PAST SUCCESSES

The method aims to develop the abilities of those in the system to retrospectively learn from their and any others' past successes. Learning workshops focus on the presentation, analysis and documentation of stories of success. This collective learning activity, in which various stakeholders take part, makes it possible to convert knowledge that had brought about positive change in the past into actionable language that can also be applied in other contexts.

In the workshops, one identifies through structured "reflection on action" (Schon, 1983), the hidden, "tacit," knowledge of each of the participants that contributed to their success. It is designed to produce and disseminate knowledge that will promote good practice, expand professional knowledge, stimulate discourse, encourage openness among the participants and promote the capacity to introduce ongoing learning into the system (Rosenfeld, J.M., Schon, D. and Sykes, I.J. 1995; Sykes, I., Rosenfeld, J., and Weiss.T. 2006; Ellenbogen-Frankovitz, Rousso, L. and Rosenfeld, J. 2011).

## *THE SECOND METHOD*: THE PROSPECTIVE METHOD — LEARNING WITH AND FROM A LEARNING QUESTION

The method is intended to identify actions and strategies that can help address unresolved issues. Implementation of this method requires the formulation of an unresolved issue that is important to address and impedes upon the success of the organization in achieving its goals. These are referred to as learning questions. The group then engages in reflective learning in order to identify strategies to address the unresolved issue. This method is implemented after the group has completed the first method and has developed the skills and motivation for continued learning. (Friedman, V.J. and Sykes, I.J. 2001; Weiss, T., Gavish, T. and Rosenfeld, J.M, 2007).

## *THE THIRD METHOD*: THE REFLECTIVE METHOD — LEARNING ON LEARNING IN AND FROM ACTION

The third methodology, "Learning on Learning", had been on our minds from early on in our working on the methodology of learning from success and ongoing learning in human services. While we had been aware of this being a methodology that would emerge and had to emerge after mastering the previous two methodologies, it is still one that remains to be formulated. Based on an assumption that the primary source for learning how to best learn in the spirit of learning from success is to focus on "actionable knowledge" (modes of action) which had contributed to knowingly learning from the past and thus it being the basis for doing what is to be done in the present for the future with full awareness that it is to be presented in actionable language, as it is at the heart of the quest of learning from success with its two spheres:

1. The actual learning connected to how to become effective learners, learners who are able to master the first and second learning from success methodologies. The third one is a methodology which is still to be developed and explicated.
2. The learning of how to disseminate over the years learning from success, be it via unbeknownst or beknownst authors.

To do both of these takes retrospective (re)search and learning to know how to effectively disseminate it and put it to use.

# Appendix IV
# The Components of the First and the Second Methods of Learning from Past Success

*FIRST METHOD*: THE RETROSPECTIVE METHOD — LEARNING FROM PAST SUCCESS

A learning group is developed within the organization, composed of different stakeholders involved in learning, proceeds to implement the first method.

The method is implemented in 10 predetermined learning stages:

### Stage 1 — Identification of the organizational context

Concise description of the nature of the organization.

### Stage 2 — Identifying a success worthy of being learned from and identifying the dimensions(s) of its success

The facilitator of the inquiry asks the participants to briefly describe successes they have had in the past which had promoted the mission and purposes of the organization. One of these successes is chosen to serve as the focus of the process of identifying the actions that had contributed to this success. The successes to be identified are usually the yields of professional and other endeavors

### Stage 3—Concise description of the success in "before" and "after" terms.

Description of the situation preceding the actions that had led to the success and the situation following the success. These descriptions shed light on a change that is perceived as having been successful and on the actions that had led to it.

### Stage 4—Identifying the positive outcomes (objective and subjective) of the success.

The group reflects in order to determine and define objective—and, insofar as possible—measurable objective successes and also subjective ones. The successes are examined from the standpoint of personal, interpersonal and functional experiences and system-level processes.

### Stage 5—Identifying negative by-products of the success.

Identifying negative by-products of the attainment of the change described in the previous stages, e.g., harm to people who sustained a loss due to the process or who were left behind, or actions taken that were contrary to the learners' values. The costs of the success in terms of inputs invested—e.g., money, time, and energy—are also identified.

### Stage 6—Deciding whether the success at hand is one that justifies further study.

In view of the description of the success and its implications, the group asks again whether the success story chosen is in fact worthy of being the focus of the learning process. The participants decide whether they agree to continue with the particular example or to go back to Stage 2 and choose another success story.

### Stage 7—Identifying the actions that had led to the success.

By reflecting on his or her action, each speaker is asked to describe concretely and concisely, the actions taken in the process and to do so without explanations and interpretations ("don't explain, just tell what the heck did you do", Donald Schön).

### Stage 8—Identifying turning points that have particularly contributed to the change between the "before" and the "after".

Reviewing the actions taken to identify those that may be viewed turning points in achieving the outcomes.

## Stage 9—Generating the principles of actions underlying the actions that led and contributed to the success (Stage 7).

Rephrasing the actions that contributed to the success in actionable language, i.e. in terms of learning principles, so that they may be applied in other settings.

## Stage 10—Identifying unresolved issues for ongoing learning.

Identifying unresolved issues that need further attention in and for the future.

## SECOND METHOD: THE PROSPECTIVE METHOD— LEARNING WITH AND FROM LEARNING QUESTIONS

The method begins by identifying a selected area of activities in which it is felt that changes are needed and can be put in terms of a "learning question". Subsequently, two parallel groups are set up as "learning groups," one of which studies the area in question to understand the problem and to identify possible ways of addressing it, and the second, an "action group" which is responsible for bringing about the desired change. The two groups cooperate in the learning process.

The method is implemented in ten predetermined stages.

## Stage 1—Identifying an area in which change is needed.

Identifying an area in the system where a change would promote the attainment of the system's vision via a response to a "learning quest".

## Stage 2—Choosing the participant in the learning process.

Based on the area chosen, its participants are identified: The action group and a group of learning companions.

## Stage 3—Defining the specific learning question.

The first task is to choose and define one specific issue within the broad area that has been chosen as the focus of the learning process. In line with this, the learning question is formulated that addresses a crucial and unresolved issue in the system that lies at the core of the endeavor the members of the action and learning the groups.

The learning question is formulated in the following way:

> *How can action(s) be taken on the issue X, in which the desired situation is Y, in order to attain the desired situation Z?*

### Stage 4 — Broadening the circle of participants and achieving cohesion among the participants.

At this stage additional participants may be added, whose interests and expertise are particularly relevant to the issue chosen.

### Stage 5 — Creating a set of alternative actions and choosing among them.

Raising ideas on how an alternative mode of addressing the learning question, discussing them, and deciding which of them are the most suitable.

### Stage 6 — Preparing an action plan and defining indicators of success.

Devising an action plan for the alternative chosen, selecting a period of time for its performance, and determining valid and relevant indicators for the assessment of progress and of the successful and full implementation of the plan.

### Stage 7 — Implementing the action plan accompanied by ongoing measurement and learning.

Implementation takes place in accordance with the action plan and as modified by the ongoing learning process accompanying.

### Stage 8 — Identifying the actions and principles of action that had led to the desired outcome.

Based on the actions deployed, identifying the principles of action that have contributed to the success of the project so that it can be applied in other contexts.

### Stage 9 — Reflecting on the learning process and unresolved issues.

Reflecting on the learning process to identify what contributed to its success and what were its unresolved issues.

### Stage 10 — Documentation and dissemination.

A formal documentation is prepared which relates to the actions employed, the objective indicators of success, the experiences of the participants in the learning process and any unresolved issues. This documentation is there also to share it more broadly with relevant colleagues and stakeholders as the basis for more widely disseminating the outcomes of this process and the lessons learned.

# References

August Aichhorn, *Wayward Youth* (New York: The Viking Press, 1935).
Hannah Arendt, *Eichmann in Jerusalem: The Banality of Evil* (New York: The Viking Press, 1963).
Chris Argyris, *Knowledge for Action: A Guide to Overcoming Barriers to Organizational Change* (San Francisco: Jossey-Bass Publication, 1993).
James Astor, "Some Reflections on Empathy and Reciprocity in the Use of Countertransference between Supervisor and Supervisee," *Journal of Analytical Psychology* 45 (2000): 367–83.
ATD Fourth World, Quart Monde, "Extreme Poverty is Violence—Breaking the Silence—Searching for Peace, *Final report and conclusions of the 2009–2012 Action-Research Project and International Colloquium* (Vauréal, France: ATD Fourth World, 2012).
Amilia Aviel, "Boys in a Neighborhood, Everyday Life in the Hatikva Neighborhood" (PhD diss., The Hebrew University of Jerusalem, 1976) (Hebrew).
Sarit Barzilai, Jona M. Rosenfeld and Golan Fadida-Peleg. *'Better Together' Creating Partnerships among Communities and Social Systems* (Jerusalem: Ashalim, JDC, 2014) (Hebrew).
Bruno Bettelheim, "Individual and Mass Behavior in Extreme Situations," *Journal of Abnormal and Social Psychology* 38 (1943): 417–52.
John Bowlby, *Attachment and Loss* (New York: Basic Books, 1969).
T. Berry Brazelton, Barbara Kostowski and Mary Main, "The Origins of Reciprocity: The Early Mother-Infant Interaction", in *The Effect of the Infant on its Caregivers,* ed. Michael Lewis *et al* (London: Wiley-Interscience, 1974).
Robert J. Chaskin and Jona M. Rosenfeld, editors, *Research for Action: Cross-National Perspectives on Connecting Knowledge, Policy and Practice for Children* (New York: Oxford University Press, 2008).
Genevieve Defraigne-Tardieu, "Unleashing Hidden Potential", January 1999-November 2000—UHP Seminar, Volume 1&2 (Baillet en France, ATD Fourth Word, 2002).
John Dewey and Arthur F. Bentley, *Knowing and the Known* (Boston: Beacon Press, 1949).
Hazel Douglas, *Containment and Reciprocity* (London and New York: Routledge, 2007).
Thomas S. Eliot, *The Four Quartets* (New York: Harcourt Brace and Company, 1943).
Sarit Ellenbogen-Frankovits, Lily Rousso and Jona M. Rosenfeld, *See, Do, See & Renew: How to Disseminate and Implement Educational Experiments and Initiatives in Israel's Educational System—The Method of Learning from Success* (Jerusalem: Ministry of Education and Myers-JDC Brookdale Institute, 2011) (Hebrew).
Sarit Ellenbogen-Frankovits, Orna Shemer and Jona M. Rosenfeld, *Promoting Organizational Learning Processes: A Handbook Introducing Learning from Success and Ongoing Learning* (Jerusalem: Myers-JDC Brookdale Institute, 2011) (Hebrew).

Shmuel Ellis and Inbarr Davidi, *Switching Cognitive Gears from Automatic to Conscious: Drawing Lessons from Successful vs. Failed Events* (Tel Aviv: Israel Institute of Business Research, 1999).

Erik H. Erickson, *Childhood and Society* (New York: Norton, 1950).

Edward M. Forster, *Howard's End* (London: Edward Arnold, 1910).

Sigmund Freud, "The Interpretation of Dreams", in: *The Standard Edition of the Complete Psychological Works of Sigmund Freud*. Trans. James Strachey et al (London: Hogarth Press, 1900).

———. *The Future of an Illusion* (London: Hogworth Press, 1927).

———. *The Einstein-Freud Correspondence (1931–1932)*. Retrieved from www.public.asu.edu/~jmlynch/273/documents/FreudEinstein.pdf .

Victor J. Friedman and Israel J. Sykes, "Reflection 'in', Reflection 'on', and Action Science Research," in *Effective Change Management Using Action Learning and Action Research: Concepts, Frameworks, Processes, Applications*. Ed. Shankar Sankaran et al (Lismore, Australia: Southern Cross University Press, 2001).

Erich Fromm, *The Fear of Freedom* (London: K. Paul, Trench, Trubner & Co, 1942).

Helen Fry, *The King's Most Loyal Enemy Aliens: Germans who Fought for Britain in the Second World War* (Stroud: Sutton, 2007).

John Gal and Idit Weiss-Gal, *Social Workers Affecting Social Policy: An International Perspective on Policy Practice* (Bristol: Policy Press, 2013).

Judy Gammelgaard, "Through Shame to Love", *Scandinavian Psychoanalytic Review* 33 (2010): 62–5.

Tali Gavish and Jona M. Rosenfeld, *Learning from Success in Elementary Education in Netanya* (Jerusalem: Myers-JDC Brookdale Institute, 2008) (Hebrew).

Joanne Greenberg, *I Never Promised You a Rose Garden* (New York: Holt, Rinehart and Winston, 1964).

Georg Groddeck, *The Book of the It* (New York and Washington: Nervous and Mental Disease Publishing Company, 1928).

Philip P. Hallie, *Lest Innocent Blood be Shed: The Story of the Village of Le Chambon, and How Goodness Happened There* (New York: Harper & Row, 1979).

John M. Keynes, *The General Theory of Employment, Interest and Money* (London: Macmillan and Co., 1936).

Michal Krumer-Nevo, (2005). "Listening to Life Knowledge: A New Research Direction in Poverty Studies", *Int. J. Soc. Welfare* 14 (2005): 99–106.

Roni Mash, "The Relationship between Types of Low Status Families and the Adjustment of Their Sons—as 'Makam Soldiers'—to the Israeli Army" (MA diss., Bar Ilan University, 1987) (Hebrew).

Cheryl Mattingly, "Narrative Reflection on Practical Actions: Two Learning Experiments in Reflective Story Telling", in *The Reflective Turn*, ed. Donald A. Schön (San Francisco: Jossey-Bass, 1991).

Anne Michaels, *Fugitive Pieces* (New York: Alfred A. Knopf, 1997).

Rafael Moses et al, "A Psychological View of the Forced Evacuation of a Small Town at the Southern-Most Tip of the Sinai Peninsula as Part of Israel's Evacuation of Sinai in April 1982: A Case Study," *Journal of Social Psychiatry* 5 (1985): 31–6.

Rafael Moses, Jona M. Rosenfeld and Rena Moses-Hrushovski, "Facing the Threat of Removal: Lessons from the Forced Evacuation of Ophira," *Journal of Applied Behavioral Science* 23 (1987): 53–71.

Ora Namir, *There was Hope Too: Description of a Mentoring Project with the Jaffe Family* (Jerusalem: Brookdale Institute, 1999) (Hebrew).

Louis Pasteur, Lecture, University of Lille (7 December, 1854).

Helen H. Perlman, *So You Want To Be a Social Worker* (New York: Harper & Row, 1962).

Thomas J. Peters and Robert H. Waterman, *In Search of Excellence: Lessons from America's Best Run Companies* (New York: Harper Row, 1982).

Otto Rank, *Will Therapy/Truth and Reality* (New York: Alfred A. Knopf, 1945).

Lilian Ripple, "Motivation, Capacity, and Opportunity as Related to the Use of Casework Service: Theoretical Base and Plan of Study," *Social Service Review* 29 (1955): 172–93.

Jona M. Rosenfeld, "Non-Users and Users of Psychiatric Help: Modes of Help-Taking and Certain Characteristics of Continuers and Non-Continuers with Psychiatric Outpatient Service" (PhD diss., University of Chicago, 1961).

———. "Strangeness Between Helper and Client: A Possible Explanation of Non-Use of Available Professional Help," *Social Service Review* 38 (1964): 17–25.

———. "Serving the Collective or the Individual? - Lessons from the Wars of Israel," *Social Service Review* 54 (1980): 220–38.

———. "The Domain and Expertise of Social Work: A Conceptualization," *Social Work* 28 (1983): 186–91.

———. "Learning from Success: Changing Family Patterns and the Generation of Social Work Practice", in *Aspects of Family Life in the South African Indian Community*, ed. W.D. Hammond-Tooke (Durban: Institute for Social and Economic Research, University of Durban-Bestville, 1987): 5–28.

———. *Emergence from Extreme Poverty* (Paris: ATD Fourth World Publications, 1989).

———. "The Future in the Past: Deriving Social Work Competence from Past Success," in *How to Organize Prevention: Political, Organizational, and Professional Challenges to Social Services*, ed. Hans-Uwe Otto *et al* (Berlin/New York: Walter de Gruyter, 1992), 249–55.

———. "Partnership—Lines for Opening Practice with and for Excluded Populations," *Hevra U'Revacha* (*Society and Welfare*) 13 (1993): 225–36 (Hebrew).

———. "Learning from Success: How to Forge Actionable Knowledge for Social Work" (opening lecture at the Learning from Success Seminar, The Alice Salomon Fachhochschule, Berlin, 1996).

———. "Learning from Success—A Key for Getting 'Out from Under', or How to Forge User-Friendly Social Work," *Chevra U'Revacha* (Society and Welfare) 17 (1997): 361–77 (Hebrew).

———. "Lernen aus funktionierender Praxis: Einführen von umsetzbaren Handlungswissen für das Werk der Sozialen Arbeit," in *Einen Weg finden*, ed. Hans-Ulrich Krause (Freiburg im Breisgau: Lambertus, 1999), 9–20 (German).

———. "Savoir Partagez en vue d'un Changement: Entre Violence et Confiance" (in English: "Divided Knowledge with a View to Change"), *Overcoming Exclusion: Between Violence and Faith* 173 (2000) (French).

———. "To be a 'Good Enough' Parent": A Programme Addressing Neglect and Abuse in Early Childhood Implemented by Nurses at Well-baby Centres in Israel (unpublished) (Hebrew).

———. "The Outsider and Diversity", in *Rethinking Diversity*, ed. Cordula Braedel-Kuehner *et al* (Berlin: Springer VS Research, 2015).

Jona M. Rosenfeld and Sandra Abrams, "The Varieties of Partnerships with Dispossessed People", in *Permanent Group on Poverty and Exclusion*, preparatory document for meeting at UNESCO, with International Movement ATD Fourth World (Paris, 1980), 77–84.

Jona M. Rosenfeld and Margaret Brandt, "A Mother Whose Child Would Not Eat: Psychiatric Casework in a Well-Baby Clinic," in *Emotional Problems of Early Childhood*, ed. Gerald Caplan (New York: Basic Books, 1956), 31–55.

Jona M. Rosenfeld, Miriam Gilat and Drora Tal, D. (2010). *Learning from Success of Youth Probation Officers—An Opportunity for Moving Beyond Marginality and Delinquency* (Jerusalem: Israeli Ministry of Social Welfare and Social Services and Myers-JDC-Brookdale Institute, 2010) (Hebrew).

Jona M. Rosenfeld and Hubiya Hamis, "To be a 'Good Enough' Parent: The Contribution of Public Health Nurses to Children at Risk and their Families," in *Utilizing Research to Promote Opportunities for Arab Children and Youth in Israel*, ed. Miriam Cohen-Navot *et al* (Jerusalem: Myers-JDC-Brookdale Institute, 2003), 53–59 (Hebrew).

Jona M. Rosenfeld. and Alaine Krim, "Adversity as Opportunity: Urban Families Who Did Well After a Fire," *Social Casework* 64 (1983): 561–5.

Jona M. Rosenfeld and Batsheva Levy, *To be a Good Enough Parent: Children at Risk and their Families—An Action Learning Program for Public Health Nurses* (Jerusalem: JDC-Brookdale Institute, 1997) (Hebrew).

Jona M. Rosenfeld and Judah Matras, *Factors in the Success of Slow Starters, High Achiever Oriented Working Class in Israel* (Jerusalem: JDC-Brookdale Institute, unpublished, 1969) (Hebrew).

Jona M. Rosenfeld, Judah Matras and Lotte Salzberger, "On the Predicaments of Jewish Families in Jerusalem," *International Journal of Comparative Sociology* 10 (1969): 234–50.

Jona M. Rosenfeld and Eva Morris, "Socially Deprived Jewish Families in Israel," in *Children and Families in Israel: Some Mental Health Perspectives,* ed. Aryeh Yaros et al (New York-Paris-London: Gordon and Breach, 1970), 428–64.

Jona M. Rosenfeld, Eva Morris and Lotte Salzberger, "Twenty-Seven Socially Underprivileged Families in Israel," in *The Family in Israel: A Reader,* ed. Rivka Bar-Yosef et al (Jerusalem: Akademon, 1969), 543–659 (Hebrew).

Jona M. Rosenfeld et al, "North of Eden: The Evacuation of Ophira, Sinai," *Jerusalem Quarterly* 33 (1984): 109–24.

Jona M. Rosenfeld and Nancy Orlinsky, "The Effect of Research on Practice: Research and Decrease in Non-Continuance in a Psychiatric Out-Patient Clinic," *A.M.A. Archives of General Psychiatry* V (1961): 176–82.

Jona M. Rosenfeld, Lior Rosenberg and Frida Elek, "'When I am my Brother's Keeper': The Contribution of Professionals and Volunteers to the Residents of Gush Katif Preceding the Evacuation" (unpublished) (Hebrew).

Jona M. Rosenfeld and Eliezer Rosenstein, "Toward a Conceptual Framework for the Study of Parent-Absent Families," *Journal of Marriage and the Family* 35 (1973): 131–5.

Jona M. Rosenfeld, Eliezer Rosenstein and Marilyn Raab, "Sailor Families: The Nature and Effects of One Kind of Father Absence," *Child Welfare* 52 (1973): 33–44.

Jona M. Rosenfeld and Lotte Salzberger, "The Anatomy of 267 Social Welfare Agencies in Jerusalem: Finding from a Census," *Social Service Review* 48: 255–67.

Jona M. Rosenfeld, Lotte Salzberger and Judah Matras, *Family Needs and Welfare Provisions: Socially Deprived Families and the Network of Social Welfare Services in Jerusalem: A Study of Congruence: Final Report* (Jerusalem: Hebrew University of Jerusalem 1973) (Hebrew).

Jona M. Rosenfeld, Donald A. Schön and Israel J. Sykes, *Out From Under—Lessons from Projects for Inaptly Served Children and Families* (Jerusalem: JDC-Brookdale Institute, 1995).

Jona M. Rosenfeld and Israel Sykes, "Toward 'Good Enough' Services to Inaptly Served Families and Children: Barriers and Opportunities," *European Journal of Social Work* 1 (1998): 285–300.

Jona M. Rosenfeld and Bruno Tardieu, 2000. *Artisans of Democracy: How Ordinary People, Families in Extreme Poverty and Social Institutions Become Allies to Overcome Social Exclusion* (Lanham, Maryland: University Press of America, 2000).

———. "Enabling Institutions to Reach the Poorest," in Chapter Four of World Bank Technical Paper No. 502 *Attacking Extreme Poverty: Learning from the Experience of the International Movement ATD Fourth World* (2001), 63–93.

Jerome D. Salinger, *The Catcher in the Rye* (Boston: Little, Brown and Company, 1951).

Chen Schechter, Israel Sykes, and Jona M. Rosenfeld, "Learning from Success: A Leverage for Transforming Schools Into Learning Communities," *Planning and Changing* 35 (2004): 154–68.

———. "Learning from Success as Leverage for School Learning: Lessons from a National Programme in Israel," *International Journal of Leadership in Education* 11 (2008): 301–18.

Donald A. Schön, "Generative Metaphor: A Perspective on Problem-Setting in Social Policy," in *Metaphor and Thought,* ed. Andrew Ortony (Cambridge: Cambridge University Press, 1979).

———. *The Reflective Practitioner: How Professionals Think in Action* (New York: Basic Books, 1983).

———. *Educating the Reflective Practitioner: Toward a New Design for Teaching and Learning in the Professions* (San Francisco: Jossey-Bass, 1987).

———. (ed.) *The Reflective Turn* (New York: Columbia University 1991).

Orna Shemer and Hillel Schmid, "Toward a New Definition of Community Partnership: A Three-Dimensional Approach," *Journal of Rural Cooperation* 35 (2007): 123–40.
Adam Smith, (1759). *The Theory of Moral Sentiments* (London: A. Millar, 1759).
Roni Strier, "Responding to the Global Economic Crisis: Inclusive Social Work Practice," *Social Work* 58 (2013): 344–53.
Israel Sykes *et al*, "Collective Reflection at Work through Learning from Success," *Productive Reflection and Learning at Work* (Stockholm: National Institute of Working Life, 2004).
Israel Sykes, Jona M. Rosenfeld. and Tsila Weiss, *Learning from Success as Leverage for School-wide Learning—A Pilot Program 2002–2005—The First Method—Learning from Past Success: The Retrospective Method* (Jerusalem: Israeli Ministry of Education and Myers-JDC Brookdale Institute, 2006) (Hebrew).
Jessie Taft, *A Functional Approach to Family Case Work* (Philadelphia: University of Pennsylvania Press, 1944).
Bruno Tardieu and Jona M. Rosenfeld, *From Impasse to Action: The Forging of Reciprocity—How Allies of ATD Fourth World Reconnected Excluded Families Living in Extreme Poverty with Societal Institutions* (Paris: ATD Fourth World Publications, 1998) (French).
Jean Watson, *Nursing: The Philosophy and Science of Caring* (Boston: Little Brown, 1979).
Tsila Weiss, Tali Gavish, and Jona M. Rosenfeld, *Learning from Success as Leverage for School-wide Learning: A Pilot Program 2002–2005—The Second Method—From a Learning Question to a Learning Quest: The Prospective Method* (Jerusalem: Israeli Ministry of Education and Myers-JDC Brookdale Institute, 2007) (Hebrew).
Donald Winnicott, "Transitional Objects and Transitional Phenomena: A Study of the First Not-Me Possession," *International Journal of Psychoanalysis* 34 (1953): 89–97.

# Index

abandoned pregnant mother, 68–69
absorption, of low-income boys, 58
achievements, of "Good Enough Parenting", 70–71
action. *See* learning for action; Principles of Actions
Aichhorn, August, 50
Air Force pilots, in Israel: cadet training, 54; flunking of cadets, 54–55; Head of Air Force, 54, 55; head trainer, 55; power of collective relating to, 54; spin, 55; trainers of, 54–55
Arendt, Hannah, 114, 116
Argyris, Chris, 23, 30, 53, 73
army, 23; Menachem as patient, 24–25; mental health officer in, 21, 25, 37, 56; psychiatric social worker in, 25; psychiatric unit in, 23–26
"Artisans of Democracy", 91, 97–99
ATD Fourth World Movement, 8, 29, 39, 45, 47, 72, 75, 113; emergence from extreme poverty, 91, 95–99; International Action Seminar of, 96; learning companions, 90–91, 97–99, 110; learning for action, 103–109; learning from success, 109–110, 116; people living in poverty, 92–93; purpose of, 121–122; reciprocity and ongoing learning, 89–92; working with, 93–94; World Day for Eradication of Poverty, 99–103

autonomy, 11, 29, 38–39
Aviel, Amilia, 57–58

bar-mitzvah, 4, 9, 11
Berlin, 5, 6
betrayal feelings, about forced evacuations, 62–63
Bettelheim, Bruno, 38
Beumel, Reuven, 61
Blitz, 37
Borelli, Mario, 44, 94
"Boys in a Neighborhood, Everyday Life in Hatikva Neighborhood" (Aviel), 57
British Army, 14, 23
British Mandate, of Palestine, 14
brothers, 4, 8; Immanuel, 4, 5, 6, 7; Jakob, 4, 5, 6–7, 9

cadets: flunking of, 54–55; training of, 54
Caplan, Gerald, 26–27
"The Catcher in the Rye" (Salinger), 34
change-oriented knowledge, 53
children, mothers separated from, 37
client exclusion, 40
clients: at Well-Baby Centers, in Jerusalem, 27–28. *See also* helper and client, strangeness of
collective solidarity, 66
collective violence, 65
collective weakness, 115–116
"Colonial Social Science", 19

communism, 47
community social work, 97
complex situations, learning from success in, 113, 114
content analysis, of invention of interventions, 40–41
continuers, 40–41
contributions, of helper and client, 37
Cornuau, Bernadette, 95, 100, 100–101

Defraigne-Tardieu, Genevieve, 103, 117
dyadic therapy, 51

EDF. *See* Electric Company of France
Eisenstadt, Shmuel, 34, 54
Electric Company of France (EDF), 98–99
"Emergence from Extreme Poverty", 91, 95; EDF and, 98–99; family contributions relating to, 96–97; learning companions and, 97–99; patronizing social work relating to, 96; reciprocity relating to, 97; successes, 95; tenderness and, 98–99; Volunteer corps relating to, 95, 96
eradication: of poverty, 116, 121–122. *See also* World Day for Eradication of Poverty
evacuated families, in post-war London, 20–21
evacuations. *See* forced evacuations; forced evacuations, from Gaza Strip; forced evacuations, from Sinai Peninsula
excluded in our midst, 37, 90
exclusion, 25, 31, 39, 113; client, 40. *See also* moving beyond exclusion
exclusion to reciprocity, move from, 54, 77–81, 89–90, 91, 113
exigencies: of people living in poverty, 92–93; predicaments and, 44
experience: with learning from success, 78; in London, 17–18, 34; with reciprocity, 48–50
expulsion, forced evacuations as, 61–62
external learning companions, 124
"Extreme Poverty is Violence", 116

familial roots, of New York families, 59

families: evacuated, in post-war London, 20–21; Israeli Merchant Marine's impact on, 56–57; "Jaffe Family", 73. *See also* New York families, with burned down homes; socially deprived Israeli families
families, of low-income boys: concerned, 57–58; neglecting, 57–58; warm, 57–58
families living in extreme poverty, at World Day for Eradication of Poverty, 101–102
family contributions, poverty relating to, 96–97
father (of Rosenfeld): death of, 7; following of, 3–8; at Jerusalem German Immigrants Association, 15
financial compensation, for forced evacuations, 62
forced evacuations, 61; types of, 61; victims of, 61
forced evacuations, from Gaza Strip, 64; local authorities and, 64–65; preparations for, 64–65; reciprocity relating to, 65; religious social workers and, 65; social support of, 64–66, 76; study of, 64–66; victims of, 65
forced evacuations, from Sinai Peninsula, 61; betrayal feelings about, 62–63; as expulsion, 61–62; financial compensation for, 62; four evacuee groups of, 62–63; presentations after, 63–64; study of, 61–64
formative years 1933-1955: army, 23–26; beginnings in Palestine, 13–18, 23; social work in post-war London, 18–23; Well-Baby Centers, in Jerusalem, 26–30
Forster, E.M., 18
Fourth World Movement. *See* ATD Fourth World Movement
Fromm-Reichmann, Frieda, 10
"Fugitive Pieces", 51

Gaza Strip. *See* forced evacuations, from Gaza Strip
genocide, poverty and: addressing of, 116–117; as man-made evils, 113–117
Germany, 5–6

"Good Enough Parenting", 67; concept of, 66, 72; program of, 70, 70–71; successes and achievements of, 70–71. *See also* "To Be a 'Good Enough' Parent"
Greenberg, Joan, 50
Group Relations Conference on Authority and Leadership, 8

Hadassah Medical Organization of America, 33
Haganah, 16
The Hague, 5
Haifa, 6
Hallie, P., 94
Hebrew University, 2, 3, 33
helper and client, strangeness of, 36, 37–39; contributions of, 37; excluded in our midst, 37, 90; respect relating to, 36–37; separation of children from mother, 37
hidden knowledge, 55
Holland, 6
Holocaust, 114, 115–116; survivors of, 24, 25–26, 27, 28, 37, 38, 114–115
Holocaust Martyrs and Heroes Remembrance Authority, the Avenue of the Righteous of the Nations, 94
home visits, 40–41
hospital, 1–3
"Howard's End" (Forster), 18
humanistic pursuits, of mother, 10

Immanuel (brother), 4, 5, 6, 7
Immigrant and Children's Youth Organization, 84
individual and collective, 46, 47; communism relating to, 47; in kibbutz, 46; serving dilemma of, 46; socialism relating to, 47
"Individual and Mass Behavior in Extreme Situations" (Bettelheim), 38
*I Never Promised You a Rose Garden* (Greenberg), 50
integration: of low-income boys, 58; into Palestine, 15
International Action Seminar, 96
intervention theories, 28–29
invention of interventions, 21–22, 40, 41–42; client exclusion relating to, 40; content analysis with, 40–41; with continuers, 40–41; with home visits, 40–41; learning companions, 29, 40; motivation and capacity relating to, 40, 51; with non-continuers, 40–41; qualitative analysis with, 40–41; with tacit knowledge, 41, 49–50, 53–54, 95
Israel: return to, 42. *See also* Air Force pilots, in Israel
Israeli Defense Force, 46
Israeli Merchant Marine, 1964, 55; families impacted by, 56–57; long week-ends with, 56–57; social services of, 56–57; study of, 55–57
Israeli War of Independence, 28

Jaboureck, Brigitte, 95, 95–96
"Jaffe Family", 73
Jakob (brother), 4, 5, 6–7, 9
Jerusalem, 2, 3–4, 6, 7. *See also* Well-Baby Centers, in Jerusalem
Jerusalem German Immigrants Association, 15
Jewish Agency, 17
Jewish and Arab communities, in Palestine, 13–14
Jewish mother study: aspects of, 44; importance of, 45–46; objective of, 44; of poverty, 43, 44; presentation of, 44–46
Jewish soldiers, in British Army, 14
Joint Distribution Committee, 73

Kadima, 4–5
Katz, Elihu, 34, 41–42
"kenn's noch Mutti", 4
kibbutz, 16–17, 20, 46
Kibbutz Ginossar, 3
Kibbutz Movement, 17
"The King's Most Loyal Enemy Aliens: Germans who Fought for Britain in the Second World War", 14
Knesset, World Day for Eradication of Poverty at, 99, 102–103
knowledge: change-oriented, 53; hidden, 55; tacit, 41, 49–50, 53–54, 95
Krim, Alaine, 58–61

Land of Zion, 7, 9
Lasker Mental Health and Child Guidance Clinic, 26, 33
learning: ongoing, 36, 50, 78; reciprocal, 97–98; reflection-based, 66, 68, 79–80. *See also* social work, learning the craft of
learning companions, 29, 40, 90–91, 97, 110; craft of, 98; external, 124; families working with, 98–99
learning for action, 103, 108–109; Pacheco's story, 108; Samy's story, 103–104; seminar on, 103–108
learning from success, 53, 90, 96; Air Force pilots, in Israel, 54–55; with ATD Fourth World Movement, 109–110, 116; in complex situations, 113, 114; contribution of, 72; experience with, 78; forced evacuations, 61–66; Israeli Merchant Marine, 1964, 55–57; low-income boys mobility, 57–58; methodologies for, 53; New York families, 58–61; nurses, in Well-Baby Centers, 66–70; reflective ongoing, 109–110; at School of Social Service Administration, 36, 37, 49; serving socially deprived Israeli families, 72–75; under-served relating to, 60, 69, 74, 74–75. *See also* Unit for Learning from Success and Ongoing Learning in Human Services
learning from success, methods for, 78, 124–125; prospective, 128; reflective, 128; retrospective, 127
learning methods: for Unit for Learning from Success and Ongoing Learning in Human Services, 124–125. *See also* learning from success, methods for; moving beyond exclusion, learning methods for
learning stages: of prospective method, 131–132; of retrospective method, 129–131
"Lest Innocent Blood be Shed" (Hallie), 94
Levin, Ezra, 34, 41–42
Lissak, Moshe, 54
London, 17–18; experience in, 17–18, 34. *See also* social work, in post-war London

London Matriculation, 17
London School of Economics and Political Science, 17, 33, 34
low-income boys: absorption of, 58; from concerned families, 57–58; mobility of, 57–58; from neglecting families, 57–58; PhD thesis about, 57–58; social integration of, 58; from warm families, 57–58

Magenpfoertnerkrampf. *See* pyloric stenosis
Manheim, Bilha, 55–56, 75
man-made evils, genocide and poverty as, 113–117
Mann, Thomas, 113
Masurel, Bruno, 95, 96
Matras, Yehuda, 43, 92
Menachem (patient), 24–25
mental health officer, in army, 21, 25, 37, 56
mental health social worker, 21
Military Transit Camp, 23
mobility, of low-income boys, 57–58
Morris, Eva, 92
Moses, Rafael, 61
Moses, Rena, 61
mother (of Rosenfeld), 1, 2, 4, 6, 7–8; background of, 8–9; characteristics of, 9; humanistic pursuits of, 10; ways of, 8–11, 11
"A Mother whose Child would not Eat", 26
mothers: children separated from, 37; of New York families, with burned down homes, 59, 60. *See also* abandoned pregnant mother; Jewish mother study; self-emancipated Bedouin mother
motivation and capacity, 40, 51
moving beyond exclusion, 28, 42–43, 43–46, 54; with generosity, 79; at Paul Baerwald School of Social Work, 43; personal abilities for, 79; practices for, 79–80; to reciprocity, 54, 77–81, 89–90, 91, 113; settings for, 79, 79–80
moving beyond exclusion, learning methods for, 79, 80; prospective, 80, 124–125; reflective, 80, 125; retrospective, 80, 124
music, 39, 51

Myers-JDC-Brookdale Institute, 53, 72, 73, 75, 123–125

Namir, Ora, 73–74
Nazis, 5
New York families, with burned down homes: familial roots relating to, 59; family relationships of, 59; improving lives of, 59; by landlords, 58–59; mothers of, 59, 60; study of, 58–61; successes of, 58–61
non-continuers, 40–41
nurses, in Well-Baby Centers, in Jerusalem, 29–30; "good enough parenting" and, 66, 67; impasse relating to, 67–68; learning from success and, 66–70; ongoing program of, 66–67; partnerships with, 67–68; reflection-based learning of, 66, 68; self-emancipated Bedouin mother, 69–70, 76

ongoing learning, 36, 50, 78. *See also* Unit for Learning from Success and Ongoing Learning in Human Services
"Onkel Karl", 14
organizations, with Unit for Learning from Success and Ongoing Learning in Human Services, 123
origins: Caput, 6; father to follow, 3–8; pyloric stenosis, 1; six weeks in hospital, 1–3; ways of my mother, 8–11, 11
Orthogenic School, 38
"Out From Under", 72–75

Pacheco, Nixon, 108
Palestine, 3–4, 5–6, 7; beginnings in, 13–18, 23; as British mandate, 14; integration into, 15; Jewish and Arab communities in, 13–14; loyal outsider in, 15; privileged life in, 15; struggle of, 13; travel in, 16
Palestinian displacement, 13
parent-child services, at Well-Baby Centers, 30
parents: influence of, 48; support of, 15; Zionism of, 15, 48
partners, 39, 40, 44, 45, 47, 48, 79

partnerships, with nurses, 67–68
patronizing social work, 96
Paul Baerwald School of Social Work, at Hebrew University: moving beyond exclusion at, 43; study at, 43–46; tasks at, 43; teaching at, 42–43; work for under-served at, 43
people living in poverty: exigencies of, 92–93; predicaments of, 92–93; study about, 92–93
Permanent Volunteer Corps, 95, 96, 100, 103
PhD thesis, 37, 40, 41–42; of Aviel, 57–58
positive deviance, 38, 58, 72
poverty: eradication of, 116, 121–122; Jewish mother study of, 43, 44. *See also* "Emergence from Extreme Poverty"; genocide, poverty and; people living in poverty; World Day for Eradication of Poverty
power of collective, 54
predicaments: exigencies and, 44; of people living in poverty, 92–93
present and past, separation of, 26
preventive programs power, 30
Principles of Actions, 53, 74, 98
prospective method: for learning from success, 128; learning stages of, 131–132; for moving beyond exclusion, 80, 124–125
psychiatric social worker, in army, 25
psychiatric unit, in army, 23–26
psychoanalysis, 10–11, 15, 48, 48–51
psychotherapy, 39, 41, 48–51, 114–115
Purim, 73, 76
pyloric stenosis, 1

qualitative analysis, of invention of interventions, 40–41

Ramot, Benjamin, 14
Rank, Otto, 39
reciprocal learning, 97–98
reciprocity, 2, 8, 15–16, 39, 47; definition of, 48; "Emergence from Extreme Poverty" and, 97; emphasis on, 51; evolving from, 83–87; with forced evacuations, from Gaza Strip, 65; gratitude relating to, 49; ideas of, 47,

65; initiating and introducing of, 77–81, 89–92, 113–114; move from exclusion to, 54, 77–81, 89–90, 113; ongoing learning and, 89–92; personal experience with, 48–50; psychoanalysis and, 48–51; psychotherapy and, 48–51; quest for, 48; with Roberts, Elizabeth, 2; under-served relating to, 90, 92, 99
reciprocity-based learning, 78
reciprocity-based transactions, 77, 90
reflection-based learning, 66, 68, 79–80
reflective in/on action, 43, 74, 75
reflective learning, 95
reflective method: for learning from success, 128; for moving beyond exclusion, 80, 125
reflective ongoing learning from success, 109–110
"Reflective Practice", 75
religious social workers, 65
respect, with helper and client, 36–37
retrospective method: for learning from success, 127; learning stages of, 129–131; for moving beyond exclusion, 80, 124
Roberts, Elizabeth, 2–3, 4
Roosevelt, Eleanor, 47
Rosenstein, Eliezer, 54, 55–56
Rosney, George, 14

Salinger, J.D., 34
salonfaehig, 3, 11
Samy's story, 103–104
Saturday Boycott Day, 5
Schön, Donald, 43, 53, 73, 74, 75, 95, 98
School of Social Service Administration, University of Chicago, 33–34, 35; learning from success at, 36, 37, 49; ongoing learning at, 36, 50; staff at, 35–36, 37–38; study at, 35; at University of Chicago, 33, 34, 35, 37–38
School of Social Work, at Columbia University, 58
school years, 15, 16
self-emancipated Bedouin mother, 69–70, 76
seminars, 96, 103–108

separation: of children from mother, 37; of present and past, 26
"Serving the Individual and the Collective: Lessons from the Wars of Israel", 25, 46
Sinai Peninsula. *See* forced evacuations, from Sinai Peninsula
social activist, 49
social integration, of low-income boys, 58
socialism, 47
socially deprived Israeli families: Namir's writing about, 73–74; Schön relating to, 72–75; serving of, 72–75; tenderness of, 74, 76
social services, of Israeli Merchant Marine, 56–57
social support, of forced evacuations, from Gaza Strip, 64–66, 76
social work: community, 97; patronizing, 96. *See also* Paul Baerwald School of Social Work, at Hebrew University; School of Social Service Administration, University of Chicago; School of Social Work, at Columbia University
social work, in post-war London, 18; choice of, 18–19; encouragement of, 21–22; with evacuated families, 20–21; joint ventures relating to, 22; mental health social worker, 21; multiple challenges of, 22–23; of students, 19; studies of, 19–21; of teachers, 19
social work, learning the craft of: helper and client, 36–39; individual and collective, 46–47; introduction to, 33–35; invention of interventions, 40–42; learning the craft of social work in, 33–35; reciprocity, 47–51; School of Social Service Administration in, 33, 35–36; under-served relating to, 36, 41, 42, 43, 48. *See also* moving beyond exclusion
social workers, 21, 25, 65
stakeholders, 47, 67, 90–91
students, of social work, in post-war London, 19
studies: of forced evacuations, from Gaza Strip, 64–66; of forced evacuations, from Sinai Peninsula, 61–64; of Israeli

Merchant Marine, 1964, 55–57; of New York families, with burned down homes, 58–61; at Paul Baerwald School of Social Work, at Hebrew University, 43–46; of people living in poverty, 92–93; at School of Social Service Administration, 35; of social work, in post-war London, 19–21. *See also* Jewish mother study
"Study of the Long Week-End", 56
successes, 95; and achievements, of "Good Enough Parenting", 70–71. *See also* learning from success
survivors, of Holocaust, 24, 25–26, 27, 28, 37, 38, 114–115

tacit knowledge, 41, 49–50, 53–54, 95
"Tante Liesel", 14
Tapori, 102
Tardieu, Bruno, 98, 103
Tavistock Institute of Human Relations, 34, 37
teachers, of social work, in post-war London, 19
teaching, at Paul Baerwald School of Social Work, 42–43
tenderness, 74, 76, 98–99
"To Be a 'Good Enough' Parent", 30, 66–72
trainers, of Air Force cadets, 54–55
transference, 51
travel, in Palestine, 16
Trocmé, Andre, 94
Tu B'shvat, 5

under-served, x, 22, 78, 79; craft of social work relating to, 36, 41, 42, 43, 48; learning from success relating to, 60, 69, 74, 74–75; reciprocity relating to, 90, 92, 99
Unit for Learning from Success and Ongoing Learning in Human Services, xiv; guidelines for, 124–125; learning methods for, 124–125; objectives of, 124; organizations working with, 123; purpose of, 123; strategy of, 125
University of Chicago, 33, 34, 35, 37–38

victims, of forced evacuations, 61, 65
Volunteer Corps. *See* Permanent Volunteer Corps

War of Independence, 23
*Wayward Youth* (Aichhorn), 50
Well-Baby Centers, in Jerusalem, 3, 26–27, 31, 33; clients in, 27–28; intervention theories, 28–29; nurses in, 29–30, 66–72; parent-child services in, 30; preventive programs power, 30
"Why War?", 114
World Day for Eradication of Poverty, 99–101; families living in extreme poverty at, 101–102; importance of, 102; in Knesset, 99, 102–103
Wresinski, Joseph: as founder of ATD, 44–45, 47, 99, 100, 116, 121; way he was treated, 93–94; words of, 101, 102

Yom Kippur War, 85
Youth Aliya, 84

Zionism, 3–4, 5, 8, 9; of father, 14; of parents, 15, 48
Zionist, 3, 4–5, 6, 11

www.ingramcontent.com/pod-product-compliance
Lightning Source LLC
Chambersburg PA
CBHW020125240426
43673CB00038B/601